CHILDHOOD IS HELL

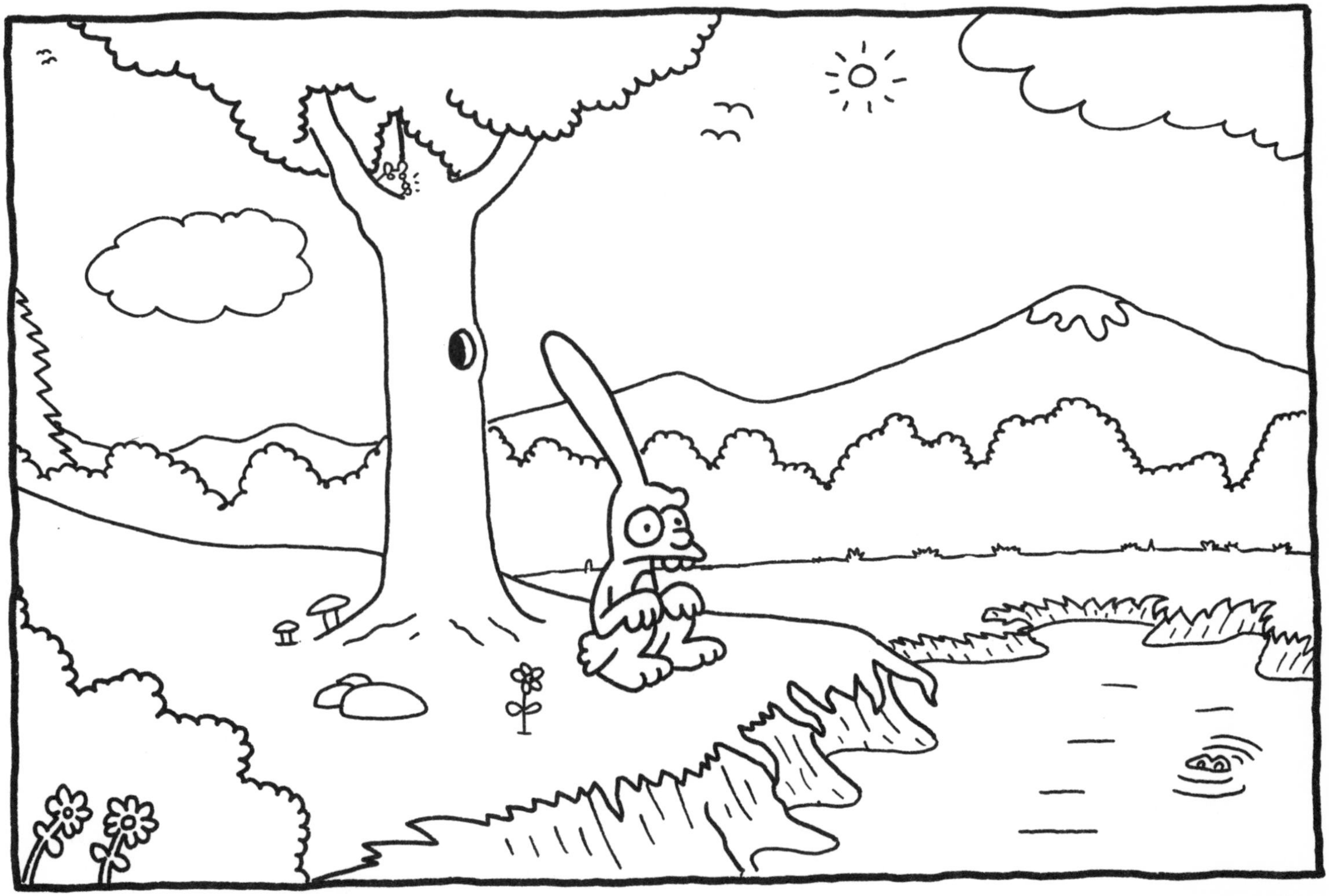

A CARTOON BOOK BY MATT GROENING

ALSO BY MATT GROENING

LOVE IS HELL
WORK IS HELL
SCHOOL IS HELL
AKBAR & JEFF'S GUIDE TO LIFE

FORTHCOMING MAYBE, MAYBE NOT

AKBAR & JEFF'S HAPPY HAYRIDE SONGBOOK
SMART MEN, FOOLISH FEZZES
MEN WHO WEAR FEZZES TOO MUCH
MEN WHO LOVE MEN WHO WEAR FEZZES
THE MAN WHO MISTOOK HIS WIFE FOR A FEZ

DEDICATED, AGAIN, TO THE RADIANT DEBORAH CAPLAN

 Published in the United States by Pantheon Books, a division of Random House, Inc., New York, and simultaneously in Canada by Random House of Canada Limited, Toronto.
I.S.B.N. 0-679-72055-3
L.C. No. 88-42761

BACK COVER DESIGN: MILI SMYTHE

SPECIAL THANKS TO EVERYONE, PAST AND PRESENT, AT THE LIFE IN HELL CARTOON CO. AND ACME FEATURES SYNDICATE: DEBORAH CAPLAN, JAMIE ANGELL, FRANK ATHENS, GARY BUSHERT, LOIS EARL, JASON GRODE, JODI INAMURA, GRACE KAMI, MERRY-BETH NOBLE, BRENDA PETRAKOS, SANDRA ROBINSON, JAMES VOWELL, AND JAN McCALL WHITMAN.
VERY SPECIAL THANKS TO THE VERY, VERY PATIENT WENDY WOLF AT PANTHEON BOOKS.
LEGAL ADVISOR: SUSAN GRODE

LYNDA BARRY IS FUNK QUEEN OF HERE, THERE, AND EVERYWHERE

FOR INFO, WRITE: THE LIFE IN HELL CARTOON CO., 2219 MAIN ST., SUITE E, SANTA MONICA, CA 90405 USA
PHONE: 213-392-1619.
FAX: 213-392-6129.

Manufactured in the United States of America
9876

First Edition

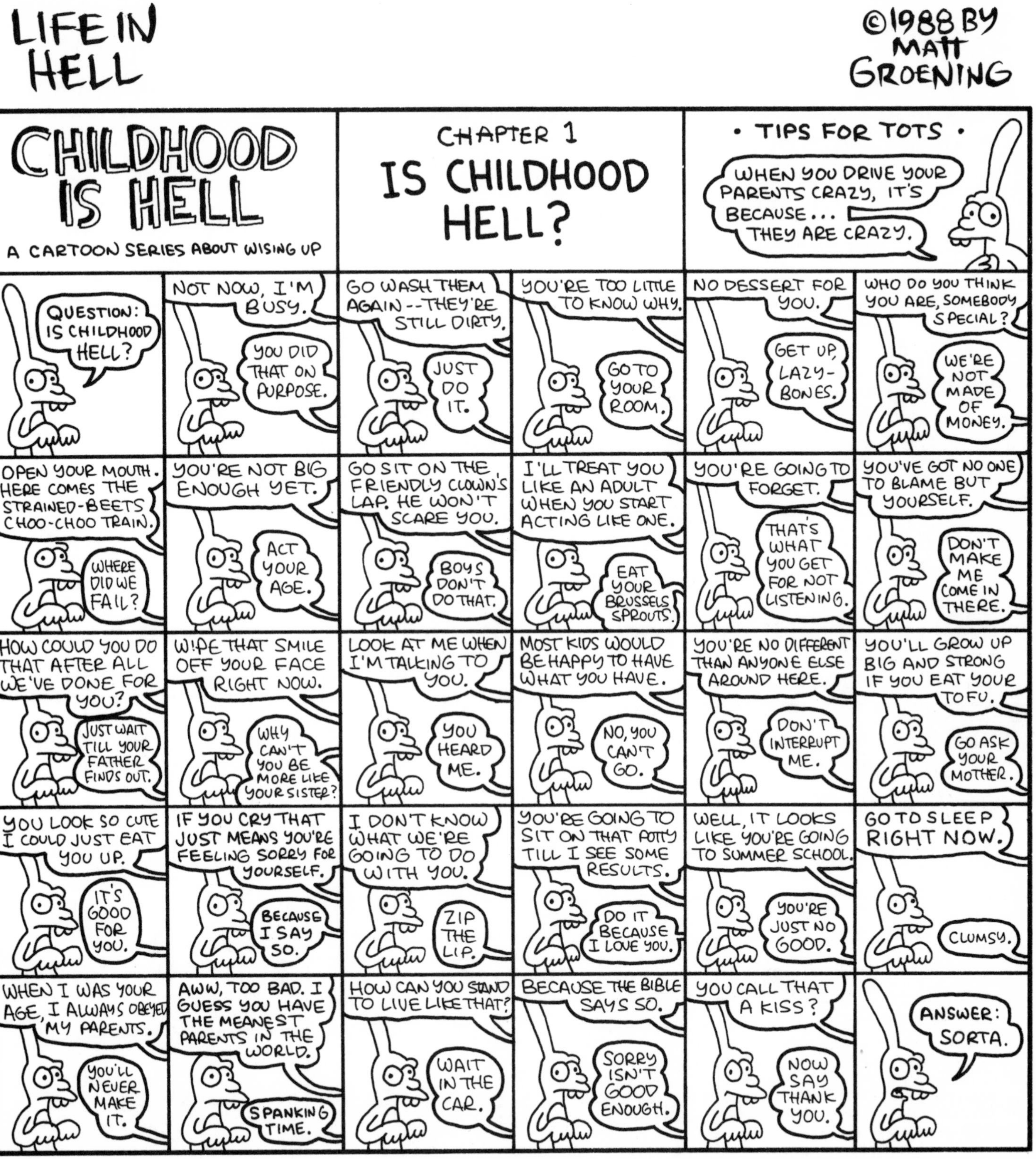
LIFE IN HELL
©1988 BY MATT GROENING
CHILDHOOD IS HELL
A CARTOON SERIES ABOUT WISING UP
CHAPTER 1
IS CHILDHOOD HELL?
• TIPS FOR TOTS •
WHEN YOU DRIVE YOUR PARENTS CRAZY, IT'S BECAUSE... THEY ARE CRAZY.
QUESTION: IS CHILDHOOD HELL?
NOT NOW, I'M BUSY.
YOU DID THAT ON PURPOSE.
GO WASH THEM AGAIN--THEY'RE STILL DIRTY.
JUST DO IT.
YOU'RE TOO LITTLE TO KNOW WHY.
GO TO YOUR ROOM.
NO DESSERT FOR YOU.
GET UP, LAZY-BONES.
WHO DO YOU THINK YOU ARE, SOMEBODY SPECIAL?
WE'RE NOT MADE OF MONEY.
OPEN YOUR MOUTH. HERE COMES THE STRAINED-BEETS CHOO-CHOO TRAIN.
WHERE DID WE FAIL?
YOU'RE NOT BIG ENOUGH YET.
ACT YOUR AGE.
GO SIT ON THE FRIENDLY CLOWN'S LAP. HE WON'T SCARE YOU.
BOYS DON'T DO THAT.
I'LL TREAT YOU LIKE AN ADULT WHEN YOU START ACTING LIKE ONE.
EAT YOUR BRUSSELS SPROUTS.
YOU'RE GOING TO FORGET.
THAT'S WHAT YOU GET FOR NOT LISTENING.
YOU'VE GOT NO ONE TO BLAME BUT YOURSELF.
DON'T MAKE ME COME IN THERE.
HOW COULD YOU DO THAT AFTER ALL WE'VE DONE FOR YOU?
JUST WAIT TILL YOUR FATHER FINDS OUT.
WIPE THAT SMILE OFF YOUR FACE RIGHT NOW.
WHY CAN'T YOU BE MORE LIKE YOUR SISTER?
LOOK AT ME WHEN I'M TALKING TO YOU.
YOU HEARD ME.
MOST KIDS WOULD BE HAPPY TO HAVE WHAT YOU HAVE.
NO, YOU CAN'T GO.
YOU'RE NO DIFFERENT THAN ANYONE ELSE AROUND HERE.
DON'T INTERRUPT ME.
YOU'LL GROW UP BIG AND STRONG IF YOU EAT YOUR TOFU.
GO ASK YOUR MOTHER.
YOU LOOK SO CUTE I COULD JUST EAT YOU UP.
IT'S GOOD FOR YOU.
IF YOU CRY THAT JUST MEANS YOU'RE FEELING SORRY FOR YOURSELF.
BECAUSE I SAY SO.
I DON'T KNOW WHAT WE'RE GOING TO DO WITH YOU.
ZIP THE LIP.
YOU'RE GOING TO SIT ON THAT POTTY TILL I SEE SOME RESULTS.
DO IT BECAUSE I LOVE YOU.
WELL, IT LOOKS LIKE YOU'RE GOING TO SUMMER SCHOOL.
YOU'RE JUST NO GOOD.
GO TO SLEEP RIGHT NOW.
CLUMSY.
WHEN I WAS YOUR AGE, I ALWAYS OBEYED MY PARENTS.
YOU'LL NEVER MAKE IT.
AWW, TOO BAD. I GUESS YOU HAVE THE MEANEST PARENTS IN THE WORLD.
SPANKING TIME.
HOW CAN YOU STAND TO LIVE LIKE THAT?
WAIT IN THE CAR.
BECAUSE THE BIBLE SAYS SO.
SORRY ISN'T GOOD ENOUGH.
YOU CALL THAT A KISS?
NOW SAY THANK YOU.
ANSWER: SORTA.

LIFE IN HELL

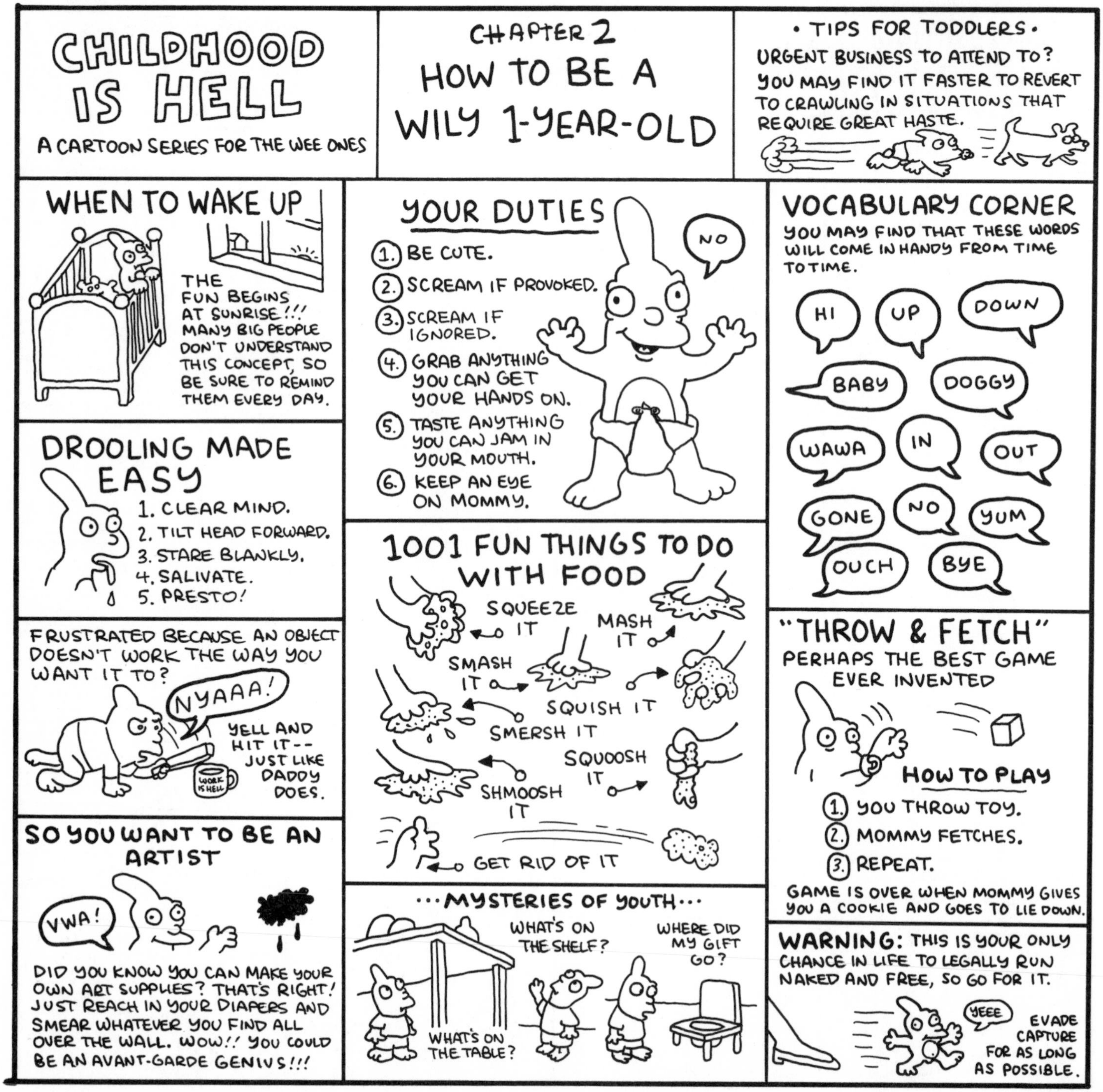
CHILDHOOD IS HELL
A CARTOON SERIES FOR THE WEE ONES
CHAPTER 2
HOW TO BE A WILY 1-YEAR-OLD
• TIPS FOR TODDLERS •
URGENT BUSINESS TO ATTEND TO? YOU MAY FIND IT FASTER TO REVERT TO CRAWLING IN SITUATIONS THAT REQUIRE GREAT HASTE.
WHEN TO WAKE UP
THE FUN BEGINS AT SUNRISE!!! MANY BIG PEOPLE DON'T UNDERSTAND THIS CONCEPT, SO BE SURE TO REMIND THEM EVERY DAY.
YOUR DUTIES
1. BE CUTE.
2. SCREAM IF PROVOKED.
3. SCREAM IF IGNORED.
4. GRAB ANYTHING YOU CAN GET YOUR HANDS ON.
5. TASTE ANYTHING YOU CAN JAM IN YOUR MOUTH.
6. KEEP AN EYE ON MOMMY.
NO
VOCABULARY CORNER
YOU MAY FIND THAT THESE WORDS WILL COME IN HANDY FROM TIME TO TIME.
HI
UP
DOWN
BABY
DOGGY
WAWA
IN
OUT
GONE
NO
YUM
OUCH
BYE
DROOLING MADE EASY
1. CLEAR MIND.
2. TILT HEAD FORWARD.
3. STARE BLANKLY.
4. SALIVATE.
5. PRESTO!
1001 FUN THINGS TO DO WITH FOOD
SQUEEZE IT
MASH IT
SMASH IT
SQUISH IT
SMERSH IT
SQUOOSH IT
SHMOOSH IT
GET RID OF IT
FRUSTRATED BECAUSE AN OBJECT DOESN'T WORK THE WAY YOU WANT IT TO?
NYAAA!
YELL AND HIT IT -- JUST LIKE DADDY DOES.
WORK IS HELL
"THROW & FETCH"
PERHAPS THE BEST GAME EVER INVENTED
HOW TO PLAY
1. YOU THROW TOY.
2. MOMMY FETCHES.
3. REPEAT.
GAME IS OVER WHEN MOMMY GIVES YOU A COOKIE AND GOES TO LIE DOWN.
SO YOU WANT TO BE AN ARTIST
VWA!
DID YOU KNOW YOU CAN MAKE YOUR OWN ART SUPPLIES? THAT'S RIGHT! JUST REACH IN YOUR DIAPERS AND SMEAR WHATEVER YOU FIND ALL OVER THE WALL. WOW!! YOU COULD BE AN AVANT-GARDE GENIUS!!!
...MYSTERIES OF YOUTH...
WHAT'S ON THE TABLE?
WHAT'S ON THE SHELF?
WHERE DID MY GIFT GO?
WARNING: THIS IS YOUR ONLY CHANCE IN LIFE TO LEGALLY RUN NAKED AND FREE, SO GO FOR IT.
YEEE
EVADE CAPTURE FOR AS LONG AS POSSIBLE.

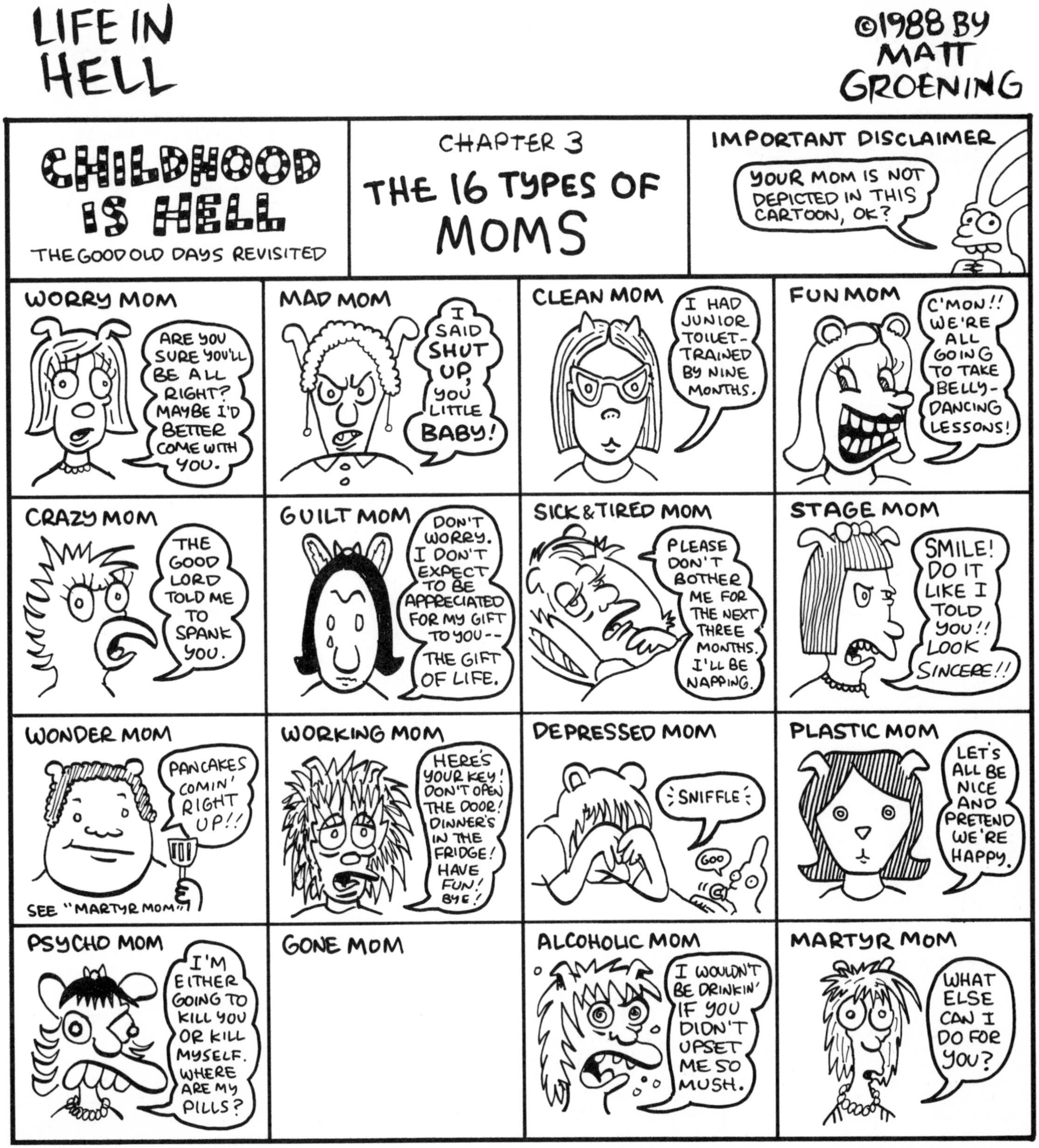

LIFE IN HELL
©1988 BY MATT GROENING
CHILDHOOD IS HELL
THE GOOD OLD DAYS REVISITED
CHAPTER 3
THE 16 TYPES OF MOMS
IMPORTANT DISCLAIMER
YOUR MOM IS NOT DEPICTED IN THIS CARTOON, OK?
WORRY MOM
ARE YOU SURE YOU'LL BE ALL RIGHT? MAYBE I'D BETTER COME WITH YOU.
MAD MOM
I SAID SHUT UP, YOU LITTLE BABY!
CLEAN MOM
I HAD JUNIOR TOILET-TRAINED BY NINE MONTHS.
FUN MOM
C'MON!! WE'RE ALL GOING TO TAKE BELLY-DANCING LESSONS!
CRAZY MOM
THE GOOD LORD TOLD ME TO SPANK YOU.
GUILT MOM
DON'T WORRY. I DON'T EXPECT TO BE APPRECIATED FOR MY GIFT TO YOU-- THE GIFT OF LIFE.
SICK & TIRED MOM
PLEASE DON'T BOTHER ME FOR THE NEXT THREE MONTHS. I'LL BE NAPPING.
STAGE MOM
SMILE! DO IT LIKE I TOLD YOU!! LOOK SINCERE!!
WONDER MOM
PANCAKES COMIN' RIGHT UP!!
SEE "MARTYR MOM"
WORKING MOM
HERE'S YOUR KEY! DON'T OPEN THE DOOR! DINNER'S IN THE FRIDGE! HAVE FUN! BYE!
DEPRESSED MOM
SNIFFLE
GOO
PLASTIC MOM
LET'S ALL BE NICE AND PRETEND WE'RE HAPPY.
PSYCHO MOM
I'M EITHER GOING TO KILL YOU OR KILL MYSELF. WHERE ARE MY PILLS?
GONE MOM
ALCOHOLIC MOM
I WOULDN'T BE DRINKIN' IF YOU DIDN'T UPSET ME SO MUSH.
MARTYR MOM
WHAT ELSE CAN I DO FOR YOU?

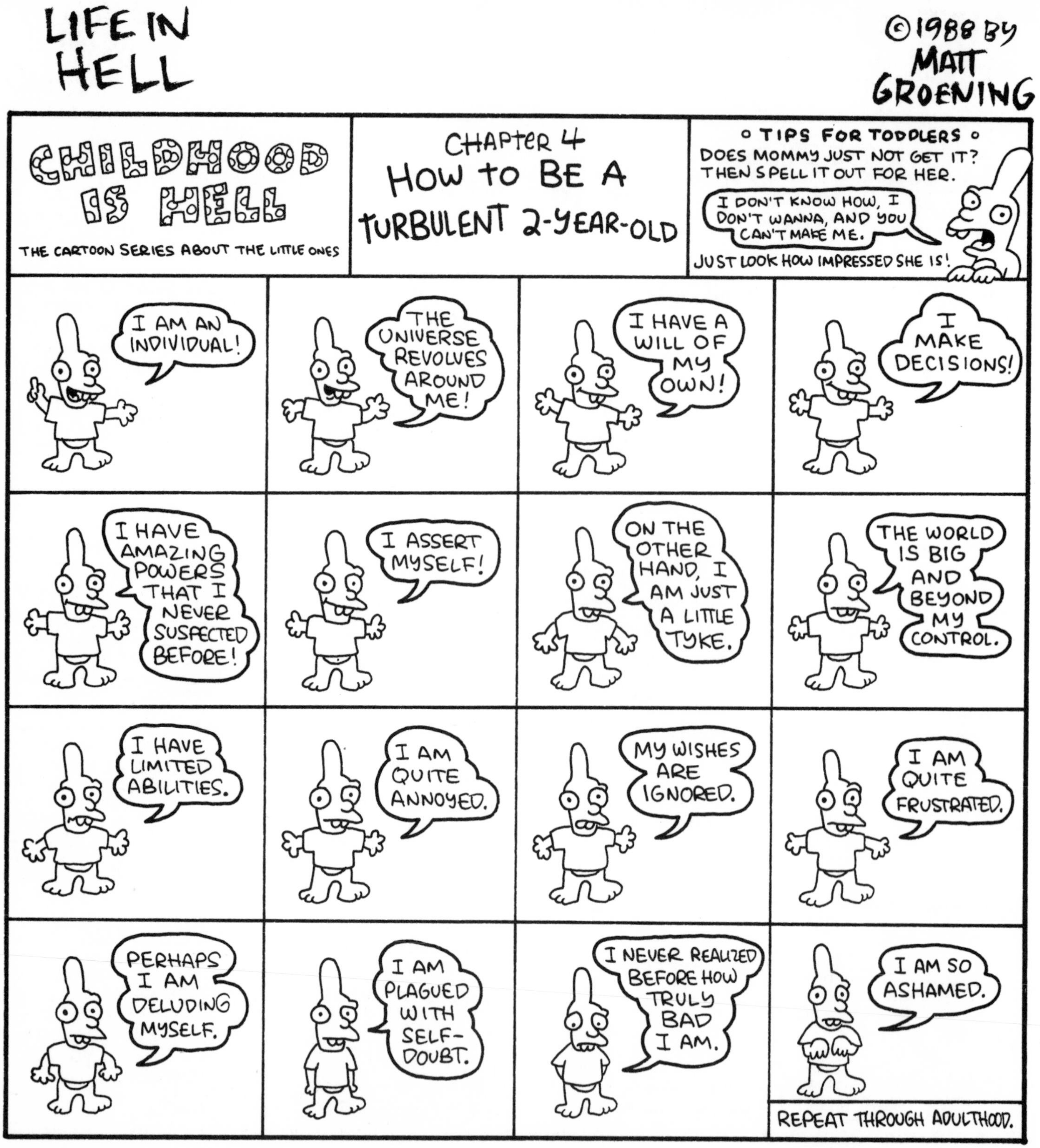

LIFE IN HELL
©1988 BY MATT GROENING
CHILDHOOD IS HELL
THE CARTOON SERIES ABOUT THE LITTLE ONES
CHAPTER 4
HOW TO BE A TURBULENT 2-YEAR-OLD
TIPS FOR TODDLERS
DOES MOMMY JUST NOT GET IT? THEN SPELL IT OUT FOR HER.
I DON'T KNOW HOW, I DON'T WANNA, AND YOU CAN'T MAKE ME.
JUST LOOK HOW IMPRESSED SHE IS!
I AM AN INDIVIDUAL!
THE UNIVERSE REVOLVES AROUND ME!
I HAVE A WILL OF MY OWN!
I MAKE DECISIONS!
I HAVE AMAZING POWERS THAT I NEVER SUSPECTED BEFORE!
I ASSERT MYSELF!
ON THE OTHER HAND, I AM JUST A LITTLE TYKE.
THE WORLD IS BIG AND BEYOND MY CONTROL.
I HAVE LIMITED ABILITIES.
I AM QUITE ANNOYED.
MY WISHES ARE IGNORED.
I AM QUITE FRUSTRATED.
PERHAPS I AM DELUDING MYSELF.
I AM PLAGUED WITH SELF-DOUBT.
I NEVER REALIZED BEFORE HOW TRULY BAD I AM.
I AM SO ASHAMED.
REPEAT THROUGH ADULTHOOD.

LIFE IN HELL

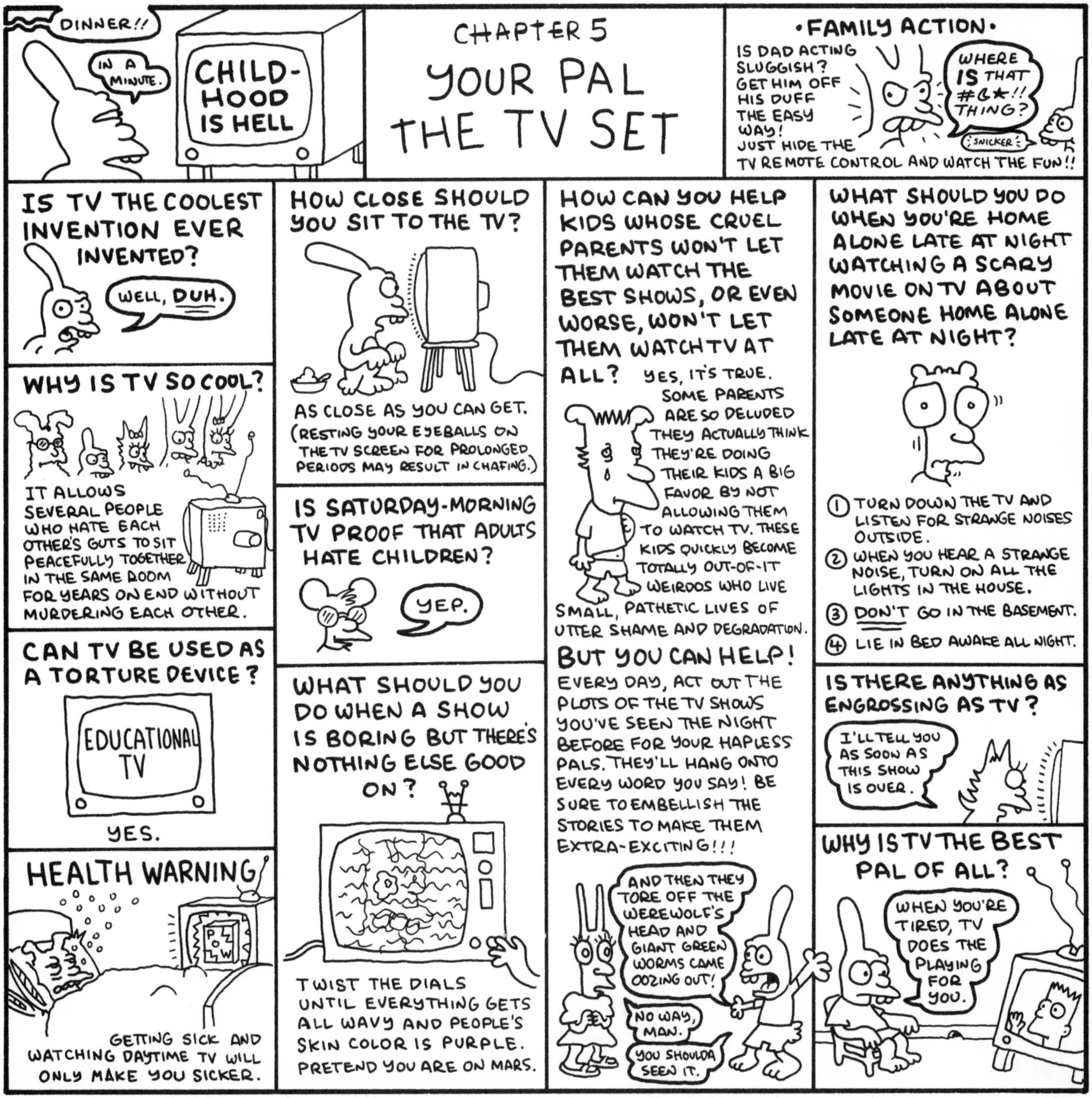
DINNER!!
IN A MINUTE.
CHILD-HOOD IS HELL
CHAPTER 5
YOUR PAL THE TV SET
•FAMILY ACTION•
IS DAD ACTING SLUGGISH? GET HIM OFF HIS DUFF THE EASY WAY! JUST HIDE THE TV REMOTE CONTROL AND WATCH THE FUN!!
WHERE IS THAT #@★!! THING?
SNICKER
IS TV THE COOLEST INVENTION EVER INVENTED?
WELL, DUH.
WHY IS TV SO COOL?
IT ALLOWS SEVERAL PEOPLE WHO HATE EACH OTHER'S GUTS TO SIT PEACEFULLY TOGETHER IN THE SAME ROOM FOR YEARS ON END WITHOUT MURDERING EACH OTHER.
CAN TV BE USED AS A TORTURE DEVICE?
EDUCATIONAL TV
YES.
HEALTH WARNING
POW
GETTING SICK AND WATCHING DAYTIME TV WILL ONLY MAKE YOU SICKER.
HOW CLOSE SHOULD YOU SIT TO THE TV?
AS CLOSE AS YOU CAN GET. (RESTING YOUR EYEBALLS ON THE TV SCREEN FOR PROLONGED PERIODS MAY RESULT IN CHAFING.)
IS SATURDAY-MORNING TV PROOF THAT ADULTS HATE CHILDREN?
YEP.
WHAT SHOULD YOU DO WHEN A SHOW IS BORING BUT THERE'S NOTHING ELSE GOOD ON?
TWIST THE DIALS UNTIL EVERYTHING GETS ALL WAVY AND PEOPLE'S SKIN COLOR IS PURPLE. PRETEND YOU ARE ON MARS.
HOW CAN YOU HELP KIDS WHOSE CRUEL PARENTS WON'T LET THEM WATCH THE BEST SHOWS, OR EVEN WORSE, WON'T LET THEM WATCH TV AT ALL?
YES, IT'S TRUE. SOME PARENTS ARE SO DELUDED THEY ACTUALLY THINK THEY'RE DOING THEIR KIDS A BIG FAVOR BY NOT ALLOWING THEM TO WATCH TV. THESE KIDS QUICKLY BECOME TOTALLY OUT-OF-IT WEIRDOS WHO LIVE SMALL, PATHETIC LIVES OF UTTER SHAME AND DEGRADATION.
BUT YOU CAN HELP!
EVERY DAY, ACT OUT THE PLOTS OF THE TV SHOWS YOU'VE SEEN THE NIGHT BEFORE FOR YOUR HAPLESS PALS. THEY'LL HANG ONTO EVERY WORD YOU SAY! BE SURE TO EMBELLISH THE STORIES TO MAKE THEM EXTRA-EXCITING!!!
AND THEN THEY TORE OFF THE WEREWOLF'S HEAD AND GIANT GREEN WORMS CAME OOZING OUT!
NO WAY, MAN.
YOU SHOULDA SEEN IT.
WHAT SHOULD YOU DO WHEN YOU'RE HOME ALONE LATE AT NIGHT WATCHING A SCARY MOVIE ON TV ABOUT SOMEONE HOME ALONE LATE AT NIGHT?
① TURN DOWN THE TV AND LISTEN FOR STRANGE NOISES OUTSIDE.
② WHEN YOU HEAR A STRANGE NOISE, TURN ON ALL THE LIGHTS IN THE HOUSE.
③ DON'T GO IN THE BASEMENT.
④ LIE IN BED AWAKE ALL NIGHT.
IS THERE ANYTHING AS ENGROSSING AS TV?
I'LL TELL YOU AS SOON AS THIS SHOW IS OVER.
WHY IS TV THE BEST PAL OF ALL?
WHEN YOU'RE TIRED, TV DOES THE PLAYING FOR YOU.

LIFE IN HELL

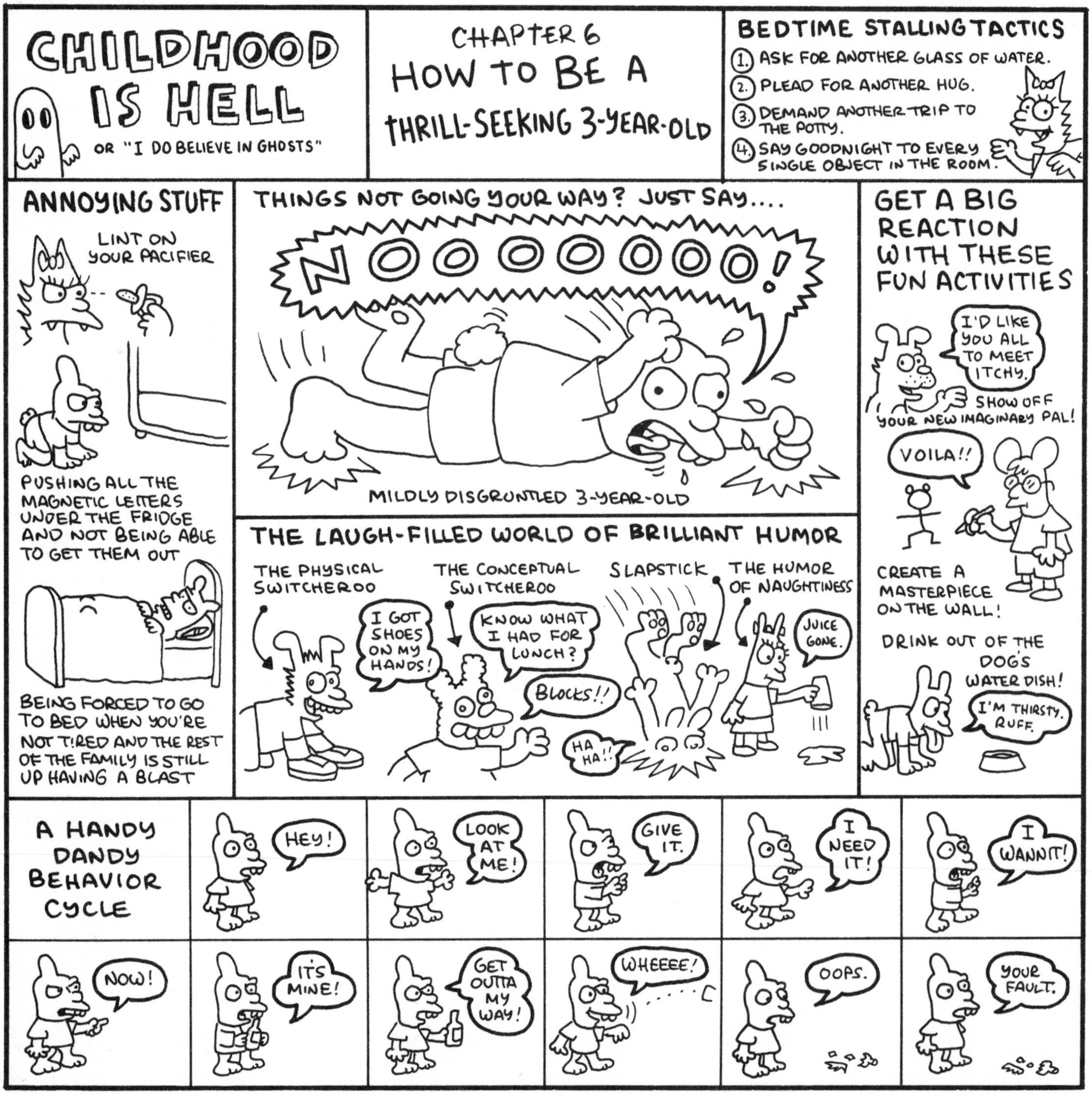
CHILDHOOD IS HELL
OR "I DO BELIEVE IN GHOSTS"
CHAPTER 6
HOW TO BE A THRILL-SEEKING 3-YEAR-OLD
BEDTIME STALLING TACTICS
1. ASK FOR ANOTHER GLASS OF WATER.
2. PLEAD FOR ANOTHER HUG.
3. DEMAND ANOTHER TRIP TO THE POTTY.
4. SAY GOODNIGHT TO EVERY SINGLE OBJECT IN THE ROOM.
ANNOYING STUFF
LINT ON YOUR PACIFIER
PUSHING ALL THE MAGNETIC LETTERS UNDER THE FRIDGE AND NOT BEING ABLE TO GET THEM OUT
BEING FORCED TO GO TO BED WHEN YOU'RE NOT TIRED AND THE REST OF THE FAMILY IS STILL UP HAVING A BLAST
THINGS NOT GOING YOUR WAY? JUST SAY....
NOOOOOOO!
MILDLY DISGRUNTLED 3-YEAR-OLD
THE LAUGH-FILLED WORLD OF BRILLIANT HUMOR
THE PHYSICAL SWITCHEROO
I GOT SHOES ON MY HANDS!
THE CONCEPTUAL SWITCHEROO
KNOW WHAT I HAD FOR LUNCH?
BLOCKS!!
HA HA!!
SLAPSTICK
THE HUMOR OF NAUGHTINESS
JUICE GONE.
GET A BIG REACTION WITH THESE FUN ACTIVITIES
I'D LIKE YOU ALL TO MEET ITCHY.
SHOW OFF YOUR NEW IMAGINARY PAL!
VOILA!!
CREATE A MASTERPIECE ON THE WALL!
DRINK OUT OF THE DOG'S WATER DISH!
I'M THIRSTY. RUFF.
A HANDY DANDY BEHAVIOR CYCLE
HEY!
LOOK AT ME!
GIVE IT.
I NEED IT!
I WANNIT!
NOW!
IT'S MINE!
GET OUTTA MY WAY!
WHEEEE!
OOPS.
YOUR FAULT.

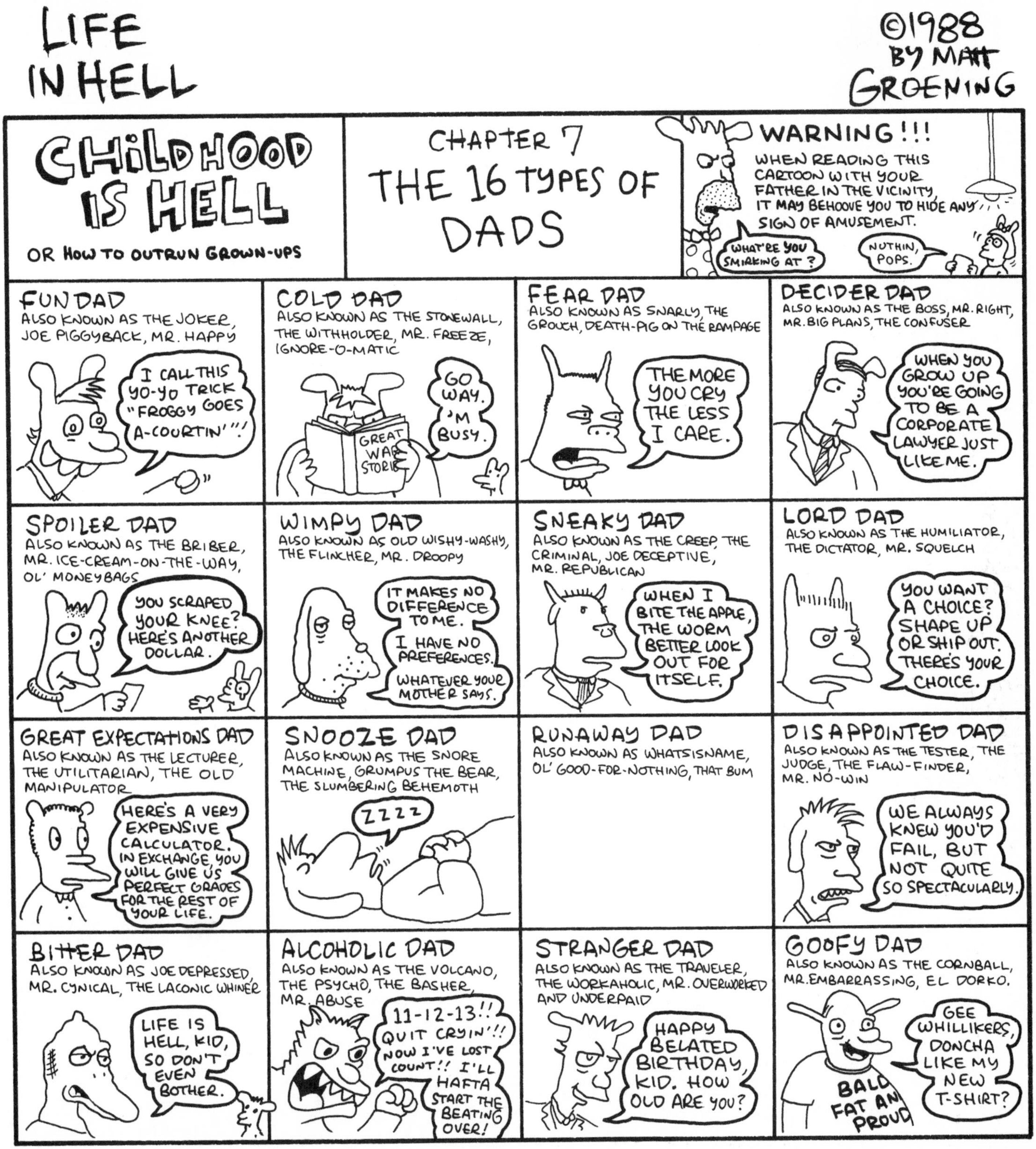
LIFE IN HELL
©1988 BY MATT GROENING
CHILDHOOD IS HELL
OR HOW TO OUTRUN GROWN-UPS
CHAPTER 7
THE 16 TYPES OF DADS
WARNING!!!
WHEN READING THIS CARTOON WITH YOUR FATHER IN THE VICINITY, IT MAY BEHOOVE YOU TO HIDE ANY SIGN OF AMUSEMENT.
WHAT'RE YOU SMIRKING AT?
NUTHIN, POPS.
FUN DAD
ALSO KNOWN AS THE JOKER, JOE PIGGYBACK, MR. HAPPY
I CALL THIS YO-YO TRICK "FROGGY GOES A-COURTIN'"!
COLD DAD
ALSO KNOWN AS THE STONEWALL, THE WITHHOLDER, MR. FREEZE, IGNORE-O-MATIC
GREAT WAR STORIES
GO WAY. 'M BUSY.
FEAR DAD
ALSO KNOWN AS SNARLY, THE GROUCH, DEATH-PIG ON THE RAMPAGE
THE MORE YOU CRY THE LESS I CARE.
DECIDER DAD
ALSO KNOWN AS THE BOSS, MR. RIGHT, MR. BIG PLANS, THE CONFUSER
WHEN YOU GROW UP YOU'RE GOING TO BE A CORPORATE LAWYER JUST LIKE ME.
SPOILER DAD
ALSO KNOWN AS THE BRIBER, MR. ICE-CREAM-ON-THE-WAY, OL' MONEYBAGS
YOU SCRAPED YOUR KNEE? HERE'S ANOTHER DOLLAR.
WIMPY DAD
ALSO KNOWN AS OLD WISHY-WASHY, THE FLINCHER, MR. DROOPY
IT MAKES NO DIFFERENCE TO ME.
I HAVE NO PREFERENCES.
WHATEVER YOUR MOTHER SAYS.
SNEAKY DAD
ALSO KNOWN AS THE CREEP, THE CRIMINAL, JOE DECEPTIVE, MR. REPUBLICAN
WHEN I BITE THE APPLE, THE WORM BETTER LOOK OUT FOR ITSELF.
LORD DAD
ALSO KNOWN AS THE HUMILIATOR, THE DICTATOR, MR. SQUELCH
YOU WANT A CHOICE? SHAPE UP OR SHIP OUT. THERE'S YOUR CHOICE.
GREAT EXPECTATIONS DAD
ALSO KNOWN AS THE LECTURER, THE UTILITARIAN, THE OLD MANIPULATOR
HERE'S A VERY EXPENSIVE CALCULATOR. IN EXCHANGE, YOU WILL GIVE US PERFECT GRADES FOR THE REST OF YOUR LIFE.
SNOOZE DAD
ALSO KNOWN AS THE SNORE MACHINE, GRUMPUS THE BEAR, THE SLUMBERING BEHEMOTH
ZZZZ
RUNAWAY DAD
ALSO KNOWN AS WHATSISNAME, OL' GOOD-FOR-NOTHING, THAT BUM
DISAPPOINTED DAD
ALSO KNOWN AS THE TESTER, THE JUDGE, THE FLAW-FINDER, MR. NO-WIN
WE ALWAYS KNEW YOU'D FAIL, BUT NOT QUITE SO SPECTACULARLY.
BITTER DAD
ALSO KNOWN AS JOE DEPRESSED, MR. CYNICAL, THE LACONIC WHINER
LIFE IS HELL, KID, SO DON'T EVEN BOTHER.
ALCOHOLIC DAD
ALSO KNOWN AS THE VOLCANO, THE PSYCHO, THE BASHER, MR. ABUSE
11-12-13!! QUIT CRYIN'!! NOW I'VE LOST COUNT!! I'LL HAFTA START THE BEATING OVER!
STRANGER DAD
ALSO KNOWN AS THE TRAVELER, THE WORKAHOLIC, MR. OVERWORKED AND UNDERPAID
HAPPY BELATED BIRTHDAY, KID. HOW OLD ARE YOU?
GOOFY DAD
ALSO KNOWN AS THE CORNBALL, MR. EMBARRASSING, EL DORKO.
BALD FAT AN PROUD
GEE WHILLIKERS, DONCHA LIKE MY NEW T-SHIRT?

LIFE IN HELL

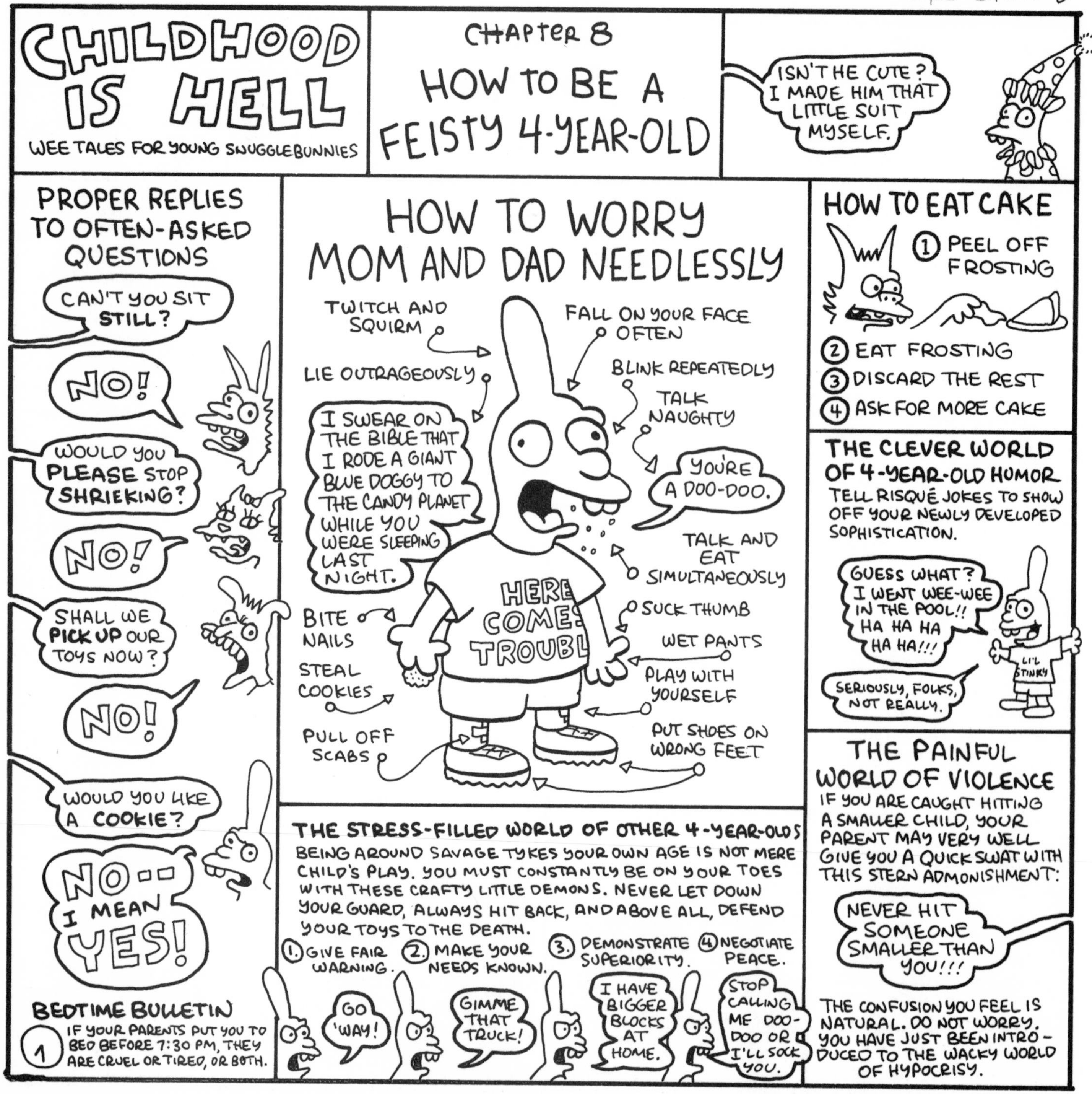
CHILDHOOD IS HELL
WEE TALES FOR YOUNG SNUGGLEBUNNIES
CHAPTER 8
HOW TO BE A FEISTY 4-YEAR-OLD
ISN'T HE CUTE? I MADE HIM THAT LITTLE SUIT MYSELF.
PROPER REPLIES TO OFTEN-ASKED QUESTIONS
CAN'T YOU SIT STILL?
NO!
WOULD YOU PLEASE STOP SHRIEKING?
NO!
SHALL WE PICK UP OUR TOYS NOW?
NO!
WOULD YOU LIKE A COOKIE?
NO-- I MEAN YES!
BEDTIME BULLETIN
1 IF YOUR PARENTS PUT YOU TO BED BEFORE 7:30 PM, THEY ARE CRUEL OR TIRED, OR BOTH.
HOW TO WORRY MOM AND DAD NEEDLESSLY
TWITCH AND SQUIRM
FALL ON YOUR FACE OFTEN
LIE OUTRAGEOUSLY
BLINK REPEATEDLY
TALK NAUGHTY
I SWEAR ON THE BIBLE THAT I RODE A GIANT BLUE DOGGY TO THE CANDY PLANET WHILE YOU WERE SLEEPING LAST NIGHT.
YOU'RE A DOO-DOO.
TALK AND EAT SIMULTANEOUSLY
HERE COMES TROUBLE
BITE NAILS
SUCK THUMB
WET PANTS
STEAL COOKIES
PLAY WITH YOURSELF
PULL OFF SCABS
PUT SHOES ON WRONG FEET
HOW TO EAT CAKE
1 PEEL OFF FROSTING
2 EAT FROSTING
3 DISCARD THE REST
4 ASK FOR MORE CAKE
THE CLEVER WORLD OF 4-YEAR-OLD HUMOR
TELL RISQUÉ JOKES TO SHOW OFF YOUR NEWLY DEVELOPED SOPHISTICATION.
GUESS WHAT? I WENT WEE-WEE IN THE POOL!! HA HA HA HA HA!!!
LI'L STINKY
SERIOUSLY, FOLKS, NOT REALLY.
THE PAINFUL WORLD OF VIOLENCE
IF YOU ARE CAUGHT HITTING A SMALLER CHILD, YOUR PARENT MAY VERY WELL GIVE YOU A QUICK SWAT WITH THIS STERN ADMONISHMENT:
NEVER HIT SOMEONE SMALLER THAN YOU!!!
THE CONFUSION YOU FEEL IS NATURAL. DO NOT WORRY. YOU HAVE JUST BEEN INTRODUCED TO THE WACKY WORLD OF HYPOCRISY.
THE STRESS-FILLED WORLD OF OTHER 4-YEAR-OLDS
BEING AROUND SAVAGE TYKES YOUR OWN AGE IS NOT MERE CHILD'S PLAY. YOU MUST CONSTANTLY BE ON YOUR TOES WITH THESE CRAFTY LITTLE DEMONS. NEVER LET DOWN YOUR GUARD, ALWAYS HIT BACK, AND ABOVE ALL, DEFEND YOUR TOYS TO THE DEATH.
1. GIVE FAIR WARNING.
2. MAKE YOUR NEEDS KNOWN.
3. DEMONSTRATE SUPERIORITY.
4. NEGOTIATE PEACE.
GO 'WAY!
GIMME THAT TRUCK!
I HAVE BIGGER BLOCKS AT HOME.
STOP CALLING ME DOO-DOO OR I'LL SOCK YOU.

LIFE IN HELL

CHILDHOOD IS HELL
A CARTOON SERIES FOR YOUNG WHIPPERSNAPPERS

CHAPTER 9
YOUR CHILDHOOD TRAUMA CHECKLIST

THE DIFFERENCE BETWEEN "A TRAUMA" AND "NO BIG DEAL"

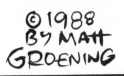

A TRAUMA IS WHEN IT HAPPENS TO ME. NO BIG DEAL IS WHEN IT HAPPENS TO YOU.

- DEATH OF PARENT
- DEATH OF BROTHER/SISTER
- DEATH OF BEST FRIEND
- DEATH OF IMAGINARY PLAYMATE
- DEATH OF SANTA CLAUS
- DIVORCE OF PARENTS
- MOVING TO A NEW CITY
- REMARRIAGE OF PARENT
- EVIL STEPPARENT
- KICKED OUT OF HOUSE BEFORE 18 YEARS OF AGE
- DAD BLOWS ALL THE MONEY ON THE LOTTERY
- PARENT ON A DIET
- PARENT ATTEMPTING TO QUIT SMOKING
- REFRIGERATOR FULL OF YOGURT
- HAVING A DORKY NAME
- REALIZING YOU'RE NOT THE FAVORITE CHILD
- FIRST CONFRONTATION WITH A CLOWN
- PUNISHED FOR TELLING THE TRUTH
- TOILET OVERFLOWING
- FORCED TO KISS WARTY OLD RELATIVES
- FORCED TO WEAR HAND-ME-DOWNS
- FORCED TO PERFORM IN FRONT OF PARENTS' FRIENDS
- BEING PUT TO BED WHEN NOT SLEEPY
- PARENTS DRIVING TOO SLOWLY
- RECEIVING UNDERWEAR FOR YOUR BIRTHDAY
- SCRATCHY NEW SWEATER
- BORING VACATION
- BEING FAMILY SCAPEGOAT

- MOM READING YOUR SECRET DIARY
- THROWING UP AT SCHOOL
- INSUFFERABLE BROTHER
- INSUFFERABLE SISTER
- BEING TOLD TO SAY "THANK YOU" FOR THE 10,000TH TIME
- BEING TOLD TO CLEAN YOUR ROOM FOR THE 10,000TH TIME
- CLEANING YOUR ROOM
- REPUBLICAN PARENTS
- FORCED TO WEAR TOTALLY STUPID CLOTHES
- FAVORITE TV SHOW CANCELLED
- DREAMING ABOUT HAVING NO CLOTHES AT SCHOOL
- CLEANING OUT CAT BOX
- PARENTS CALLING YOU BY EMBARRASSING NICKNAME IN FRONT OF FRIENDS
- WETTING YOUR PANTS AT SCHOOL
- BEING TATTLED ON
- TATTLING ON SOMEONE AND HAVING IT BACKFIRE
- FORCED TO EAT SPINACH
- FORCED TO EAT BROCCOLI
- PARENTS THREATENING TO SEND YOU TO MILITARY SCHOOL
- MILITARY SCHOOL
- SUMMER SCHOOL
- SCHOOL
- SUNDAY SCHOOL
- DANCING SCHOOL
- EARLY BEDTIME STRICTLY ENFORCED
- NOT GETTING DESSERT BECAUSE YOU DIDN'T EAT YOUR VEGETABLES
- GROUNDED

- ALLOWANCE CUT OFF
- BEING TOLD NOT TO EAT SO FAST
- BEING TOLD NOT TO CHEW WITH YOUR MOUTH OPEN
- BEING TOLD TO SIT UP STRAIGHT
- HOMEWORK
- SOCKS AS PRESENTS
- HANDKERCHIEF FOR BIRTHDAY
- PARENTS TELLING YOU WHAT YOU WILL BE WHEN YOU GROW UP
- LISTENING TO PARENTS FIGHT IN THE NEXT ROOM
- LISTENING TO PARENTS FIGHT IN THE SAME ROOM
- BEING HIT BY PARENT
- BEING KICKED BY PARENT
- SLAPPED BY PARENT
- SPANKED BY PARENT
- BEATEN BY PARENT
- BURNED BY PARENT
- LOCKED IN CLOSET
- TORTURED
- SEXUALLY MOLESTED
- GETTING LOST
- BEING CALLED "BAD"
- BEING CALLED "LAZY"
- BEING CALLED "SELFISH"
- MAKING YOUR MOM CRY
- MEETING ANOTHER KID WITH YOUR NAME
- BEING TOLD "YOU'RE JUST NOT TRYING"
- BEING FORCED TO APOLOGIZE WHEN YOU DON'T MEAN IT
- NOT BEING ALLOWED TO GO TO A SLUMBER PARTY
- BEING TOLD "I KNOW YOU COULD DO BETTER"
- FIRST TIME SEEING DEAD DOG IN THE ROAD

- FIRST STARVING CHILD SEEN ON TV
- FIRST ASSASSINATION SEEN ON TV
- FIRST REALIZATION THAT DEATH IS PERMANENT
- FIRST REALIZATION THAT DEATH IS INEVITABLE
- FIRST REALIZATION THAT DEATH HAPPENS TO EVERYONE
- FIRST REALIZATION THAT APPLIES TO YOU TOO
- FIRST GHOST SEEN
- BEING TREATED LIKE A BABY IN FRONT OF FRIENDS
- BEING CHOSEN LAST FOR THE TEAM
- NOT BEING INVITED TO A BIRTHDAY PARTY
- FIRST BEE STING
- FIRST BOOSTER SHOT
- BEING FORBIDDEN TO PLAY WITH BAD KIDS
- FEAR OF DOGS
- FEAR OF VAMPIRES
- FEAR OF ROBOTS
- FEAR OF ALIENS
- FEAR OF SHARKS
- FEAR OF MONSTERS
- FEAR OF BEARS
- FEAR OF LIONS
- FEAR OF PSYCHOPATHS
- FEAR OF NUCLEAR WAR
- FEAR OF DAD
- CAUGHT SHOPLIFTING
- BEING TOLD "YOU OUGHT TO BE ASHAMED OF YOURSELF"
- _____ (FILL IN THE BLANK)
- ONGOING NAMELESS DREAD

LIFE IN HELL

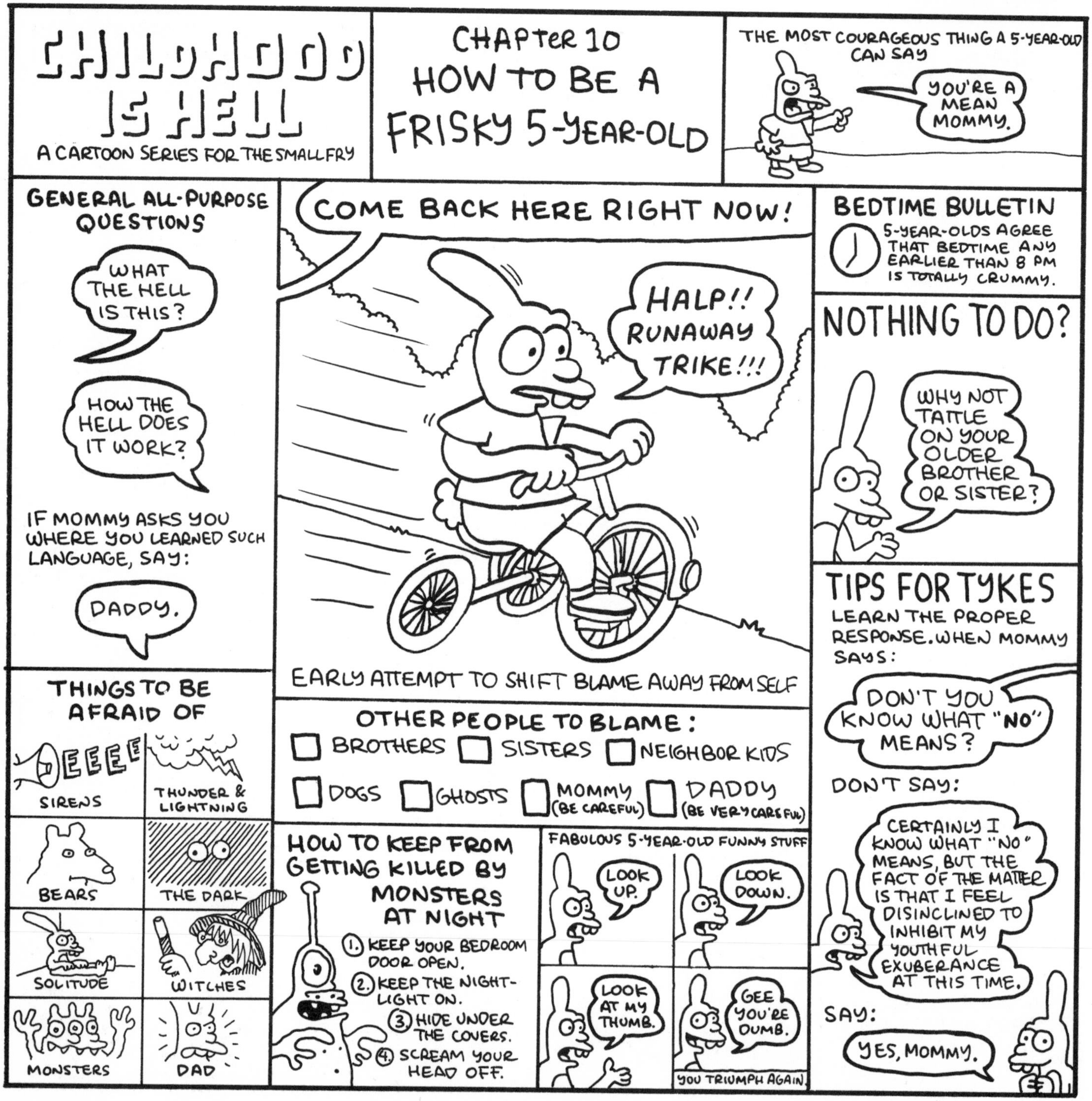
CHILDHOOD IS HELL
A CARTOON SERIES FOR THE SMALLFRY
CHAPTER 10
HOW TO BE A FRISKY 5-YEAR-OLD
THE MOST COURAGEOUS THING A 5-YEAR-OLD CAN SAY
YOU'RE A MEAN MOMMY.
GENERAL ALL-PURPOSE QUESTIONS
WHAT THE HELL IS THIS?
HOW THE HELL DOES IT WORK?
IF MOMMY ASKS YOU WHERE YOU LEARNED SUCH LANGUAGE, SAY:
DADDY.
COME BACK HERE RIGHT NOW!
HALP!! RUNAWAY TRIKE!!!
EARLY ATTEMPT TO SHIFT BLAME AWAY FROM SELF
BEDTIME BULLETIN
5-YEAR-OLDS AGREE THAT BEDTIME ANY EARLIER THAN 8 PM IS TOTALLY CRUMMY.
NOTHING TO DO?
WHY NOT TATTLE ON YOUR OLDER BROTHER OR SISTER?
TIPS FOR TYKES
LEARN THE PROPER RESPONSE. WHEN MOMMY SAYS:
DON'T YOU KNOW WHAT "NO" MEANS?
DON'T SAY:
CERTAINLY I KNOW WHAT "NO" MEANS, BUT THE FACT OF THE MATTER IS THAT I FEEL DISINCLINED TO INHIBIT MY YOUTHFUL EXUBERANCE AT THIS TIME.
SAY:
YES, MOMMY.
THINGS TO BE AFRAID OF
EEEEE
SIRENS
THUNDER & LIGHTNING
BEARS
THE DARK
SOLITUDE
WITCHES
MONSTERS
DAD
OTHER PEOPLE TO BLAME:
BROTHERS
SISTERS
NEIGHBOR KIDS
DOGS
GHOSTS
MOMMY (BE CAREFUL)
DADDY (BE VERY CAREFUL)
HOW TO KEEP FROM GETTING KILLED BY MONSTERS AT NIGHT
1. KEEP YOUR BEDROOM DOOR OPEN.
2. KEEP THE NIGHT-LIGHT ON.
3. HIDE UNDER THE COVERS.
4. SCREAM YOUR HEAD OFF.
FABULOUS 5-YEAR-OLD FUNNY STUFF
LOOK UP.
LOOK DOWN.
LOOK AT MY THUMB.
GEE YOU'RE DUMB.
YOU TRIUMPH AGAIN.

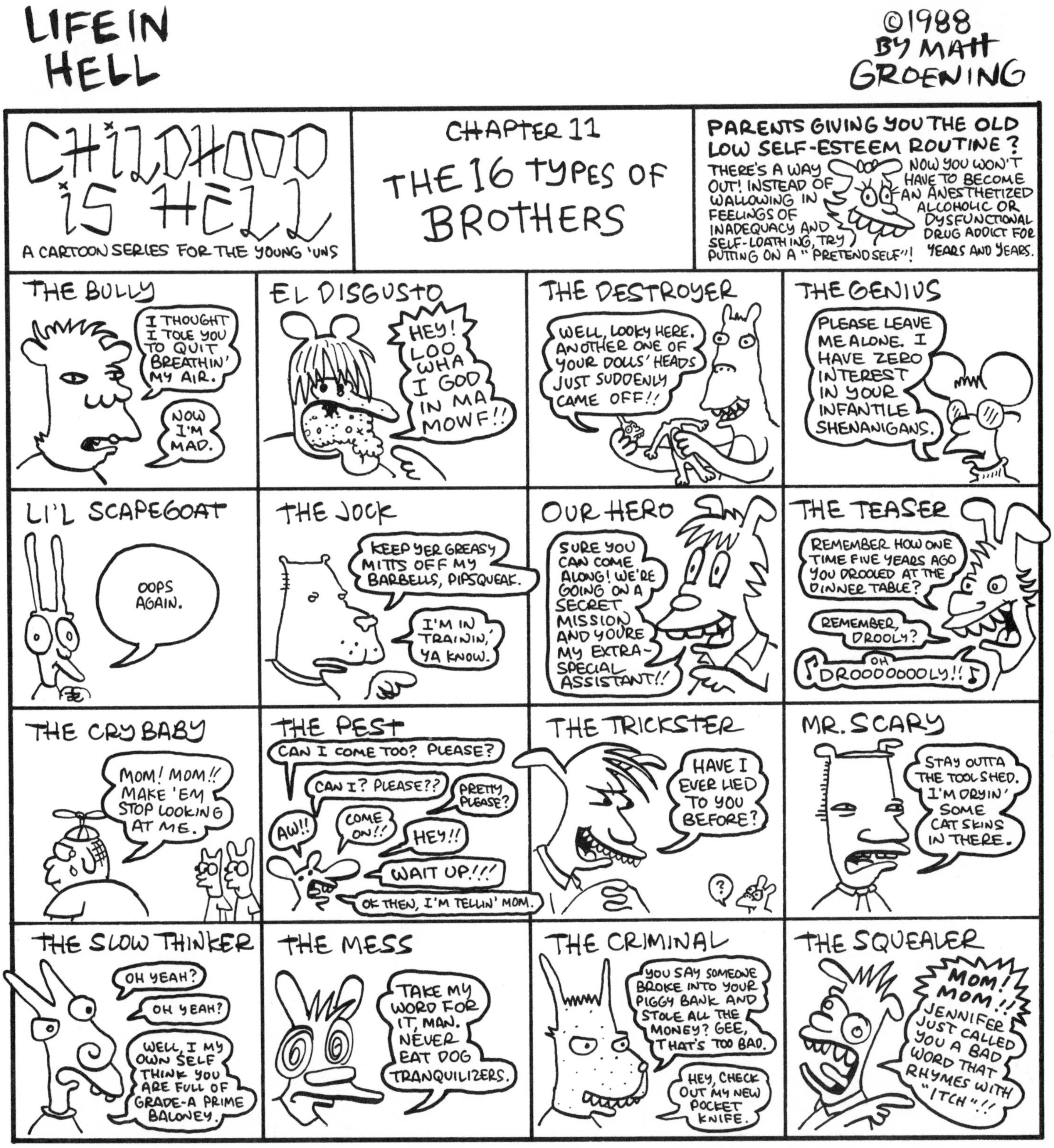
LIFE IN HELL
©1988 BY MATT GROENING
CHILDHOOD IS HELL
A CARTOON SERIES FOR THE YOUNG 'UNS
CHAPTER 11
THE 16 TYPES OF BROTHERS
PARENTS GIVING YOU THE OLD LOW SELF-ESTEEM ROUTINE?
THERE'S A WAY OUT! INSTEAD OF WALLOWING IN FEELINGS OF INADEQUACY AND SELF-LOATHING, TRY PUTTING ON A "PRETEND SELF"!
NOW YOU WON'T HAVE TO BECOME AN ANESTHETIZED ALCOHOLIC OR DYSFUNCTIONAL DRUG ADDICT FOR YEARS AND YEARS.
THE BULLY
I THOUGHT I TOLE YOU TO QUIT BREATHIN' MY AIR.
NOW I'M MAD.
EL DISGUSTO
HEY! LOO WHA I GOD IN MA MOWF!!
THE DESTROYER
WELL, LOOKY HERE. ANOTHER ONE OF YOUR DOLLS' HEADS JUST SUDDENLY CAME OFF!!
THE GENIUS
PLEASE LEAVE ME ALONE. I HAVE ZERO INTEREST IN YOUR INFANTILE SHENANIGANS.
LI'L SCAPEGOAT
OOPS AGAIN.
THE JOCK
KEEP YER GREASY MITTS OFF MY BARBELLS, PIPSQUEAK.
I'M IN TRAININ,' YA KNOW.
OUR HERO
SURE YOU CAN COME ALONG! WE'RE GOING ON A SECRET MISSION AND YOU'RE MY EXTRA-SPECIAL ASSISTANT!!
THE TEASER
REMEMBER HOW ONE TIME FIVE YEARS AGO YOU DROOLED AT THE DINNER TABLE?
REMEMBER, DROOLY?
OH DROOOOOOOLY!!
THE CRYBABY
MOM! MOM!! MAKE 'EM STOP LOOKING AT ME.
THE PEST
CAN I COME TOO? PLEASE?
CAN I? PLEASE??
PRETTY PLEASE?
AW!!
COME ON!!
HEY!!
WAIT UP!!!
OK THEN, I'M TELLIN' MOM.
THE TRICKSTER
HAVE I EVER LIED TO YOU BEFORE?
?
MR. SCARY
STAY OUTTA THE TOOL SHED. I'M DRYIN' SOME CAT SKINS IN THERE.
THE SLOW THINKER
OH YEAH?
OH YEAH?
WELL, I MY OWN SELF THINK YOU ARE FULL OF GRADE-A PRIME BALONEY.
THE MESS
TAKE MY WORD FOR IT, MAN. NEVER EAT DOG TRANQUILIZERS.
THE CRIMINAL
YOU SAY SOMEONE BROKE INTO YOUR PIGGY BANK AND STOLE ALL THE MONEY? GEE, THAT'S TOO BAD.
HEY, CHECK OUT MY NEW POCKET KNIFE.
THE SQUEALER
MOM! MOM!! JENNIFER JUST CALLED YOU A BAD WORD THAT RHYMES WITH "ITCH"!!

LIFE IN HELL

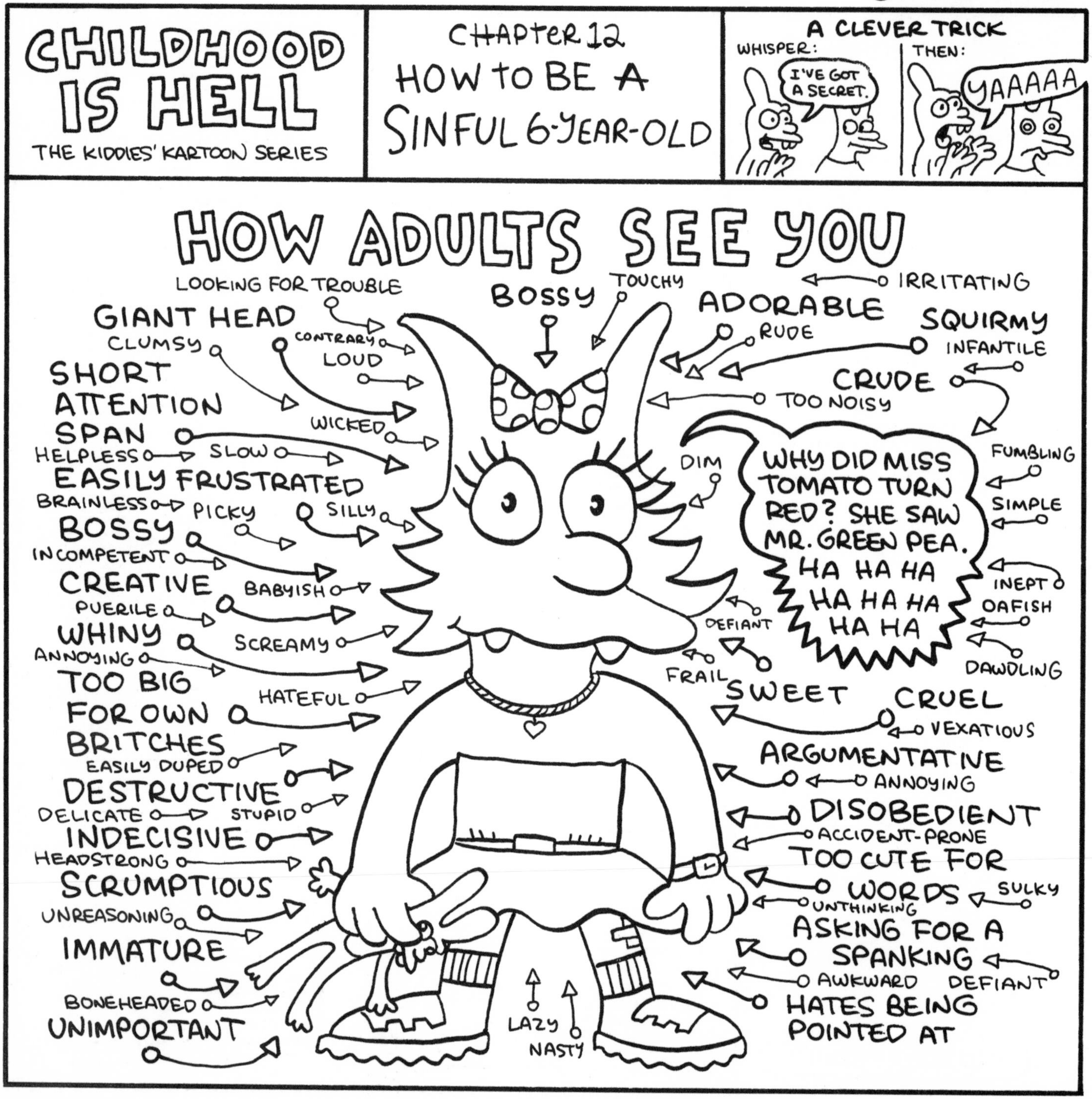
CHILDHOOD IS HELL
THE KIDDIES' KARTOON SERIES
CHAPTER 12
HOW TO BE A SINFUL 6-YEAR-OLD
A CLEVER TRICK
WHISPER:
I'VE GOT A SECRET.
THEN:
YAAAAA
HOW ADULTS SEE YOU
LOOKING FOR TROUBLE
BOSSY
TOUCHY
IRRITATING
GIANT HEAD
ADORABLE
SQUIRMY
CLUMSY
CONTRARY
RUDE
INFANTILE
LOUD
SHORT ATTENTION SPAN
CRUDE
TOO NOISY
WICKED
HELPLESS
SLOW
EASILY FRUSTRATED
DIM
FUMBLING
BRAINLESS
PICKY
SILLY
SIMPLE
BOSSY
INCOMPETENT
WHY DID MISS TOMATO TURN RED? SHE SAW MR. GREEN PEA. HA HA HA HA HA HA HA HA
CREATIVE
BABYISH
INEPT
PUERILE
OAFISH
DEFIANT
WHINY
SCREAMY
ANNOYING
DAWDLING
TOO BIG FOR OWN BRITCHES
FRAIL
SWEET
CRUEL
HATEFUL
VEXATIOUS
ARGUMENTATIVE
EASILY DUPED
ANNOYING
DESTRUCTIVE
DISOBEDIENT
DELICATE
STUPID
ACCIDENT-PRONE
INDECISIVE
TOO CUTE FOR WORDS
HEADSTRONG
SULKY
SCRUMPTIOUS
UNTHINKING
UNREASONING
ASKING FOR A SPANKING
IMMATURE
AWKWARD
DEFIANT
BONEHEADED
HATES BEING POINTED AT
UNIMPORTANT
LAZY
NASTY

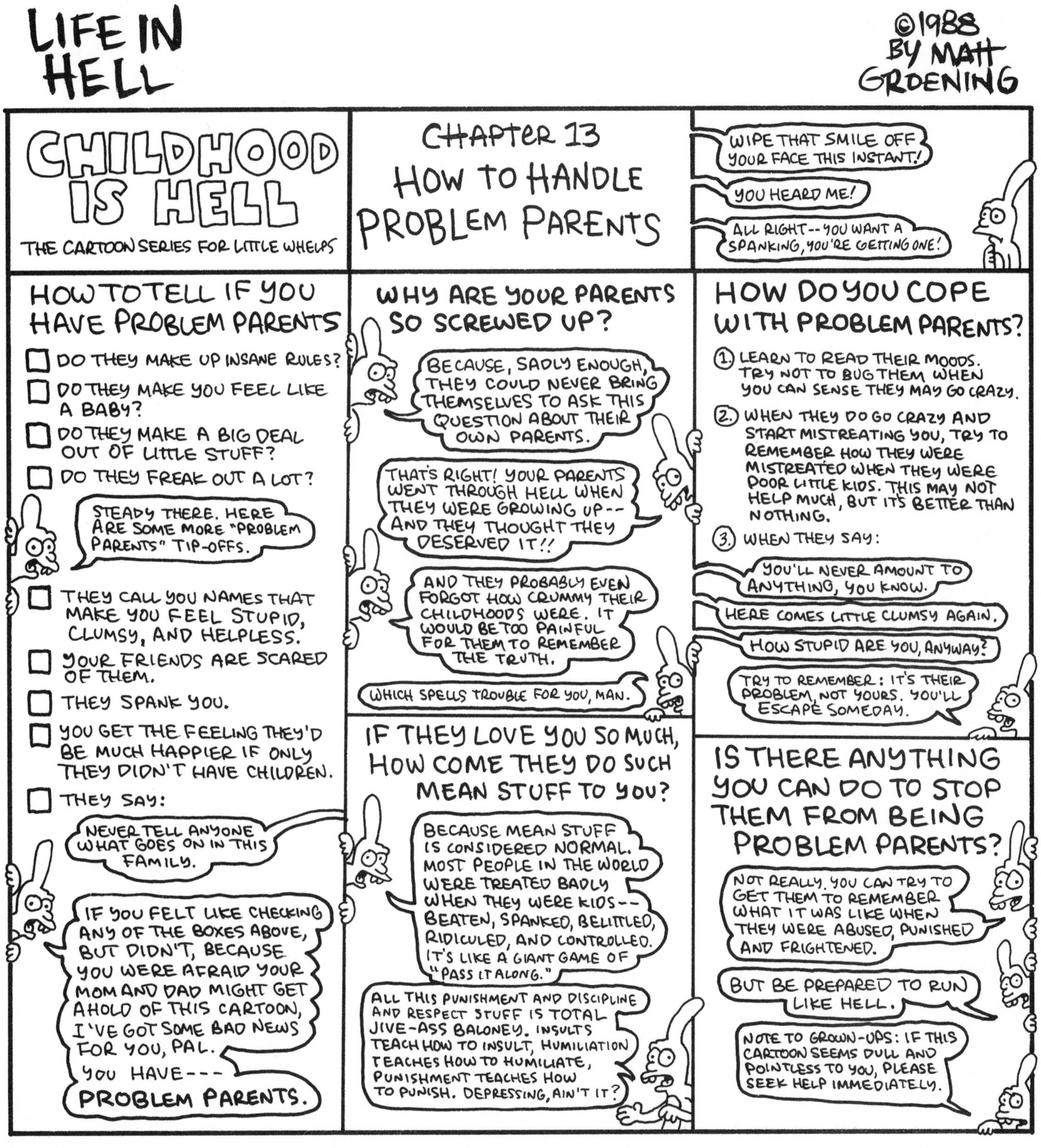
LIFE IN HELL
©1988 BY MATT GROENING
CHILDHOOD IS HELL
THE CARTOON SERIES FOR LITTLE WHELPS
CHAPTER 13
HOW TO HANDLE PROBLEM PARENTS
WIPE THAT SMILE OFF YOUR FACE THIS INSTANT!
YOU HEARD ME!
ALL RIGHT-- YOU WANT A SPANKING, YOU'RE GETTING ONE!
HOW TO TELL IF YOU HAVE PROBLEM PARENTS
☐ DO THEY MAKE UP INSANE RULES?
☐ DO THEY MAKE YOU FEEL LIKE A BABY?
☐ DO THEY MAKE A BIG DEAL OUT OF LITTLE STUFF?
☐ DO THEY FREAK OUT A LOT?
STEADY THERE. HERE ARE SOME MORE "PROBLEM PARENTS" TIP-OFFS.
☐ THEY CALL YOU NAMES THAT MAKE YOU FEEL STUPID, CLUMSY, AND HELPLESS.
☐ YOUR FRIENDS ARE SCARED OF THEM.
☐ THEY SPANK YOU.
☐ YOU GET THE FEELING THEY'D BE MUCH HAPPIER IF ONLY THEY DIDN'T HAVE CHILDREN.
☐ THEY SAY:
NEVER TELL ANYONE WHAT GOES ON IN THIS FAMILY.
IF YOU FELT LIKE CHECKING ANY OF THE BOXES ABOVE, BUT DIDN'T, BECAUSE YOU WERE AFRAID YOUR MOM AND DAD MIGHT GET AHOLD OF THIS CARTOON, I'VE GOT SOME BAD NEWS FOR YOU, PAL.
YOU HAVE--- PROBLEM PARENTS.
WHY ARE YOUR PARENTS SO SCREWED UP?
BECAUSE, SADLY ENOUGH, THEY COULD NEVER BRING THEMSELVES TO ASK THIS QUESTION ABOUT THEIR OWN PARENTS.
THAT'S RIGHT! YOUR PARENTS WENT THROUGH HELL WHEN THEY WERE GROWING UP-- AND THEY THOUGHT THEY DESERVED IT!!
AND THEY PROBABLY EVEN FORGOT HOW CRUMMY THEIR CHILDHOODS WERE. IT WOULD BE TOO PAINFUL FOR THEM TO REMEMBER THE TRUTH.
WHICH SPELLS TROUBLE FOR YOU, MAN.
IF THEY LOVE YOU SO MUCH, HOW COME THEY DO SUCH MEAN STUFF TO YOU?
BECAUSE MEAN STUFF IS CONSIDERED NORMAL. MOST PEOPLE IN THE WORLD WERE TREATED BADLY WHEN THEY WERE KIDS-- BEATEN, SPANKED, BELITTLED, RIDICULED, AND CONTROLLED. IT'S LIKE A GIANT GAME OF "PASS IT ALONG."
ALL THIS PUNISHMENT AND DISCIPLINE AND RESPECT STUFF IS TOTAL JIVE-ASS BALONEY. INSULTS TEACH HOW TO INSULT, HUMILIATION TEACHES HOW TO HUMILIATE, PUNISHMENT TEACHES HOW TO PUNISH. DEPRESSING, AIN'T IT?
HOW DO YOU COPE WITH PROBLEM PARENTS?
(1) LEARN TO READ THEIR MOODS. TRY NOT TO BUG THEM WHEN YOU CAN SENSE THEY MAY GO CRAZY.
(2) WHEN THEY DO GO CRAZY AND START MISTREATING YOU, TRY TO REMEMBER HOW THEY WERE MISTREATED WHEN THEY WERE POOR LITTLE KIDS. THIS MAY NOT HELP MUCH, BUT IT'S BETTER THAN NOTHING.
(3) WHEN THEY SAY:
YOU'LL NEVER AMOUNT TO ANYTHING, YOU KNOW.
HERE COMES LITTLE CLUMSY AGAIN.
HOW STUPID ARE YOU, ANYWAY?
TRY TO REMEMBER: IT'S THEIR PROBLEM, NOT YOURS. YOU'LL ESCAPE SOMEDAY.
IS THERE ANYTHING YOU CAN DO TO STOP THEM FROM BEING PROBLEM PARENTS?
NOT REALLY. YOU CAN TRY TO GET THEM TO REMEMBER WHAT IT WAS LIKE WHEN THEY WERE ABUSED, PUNISHED AND FRIGHTENED.
BUT BE PREPARED TO RUN LIKE HELL.
NOTE TO GROWN-UPS: IF THIS CARTOON SEEMS DULL AND POINTLESS TO YOU, PLEASE SEEK HELP IMMEDIATELY.

LIFE IN HELL

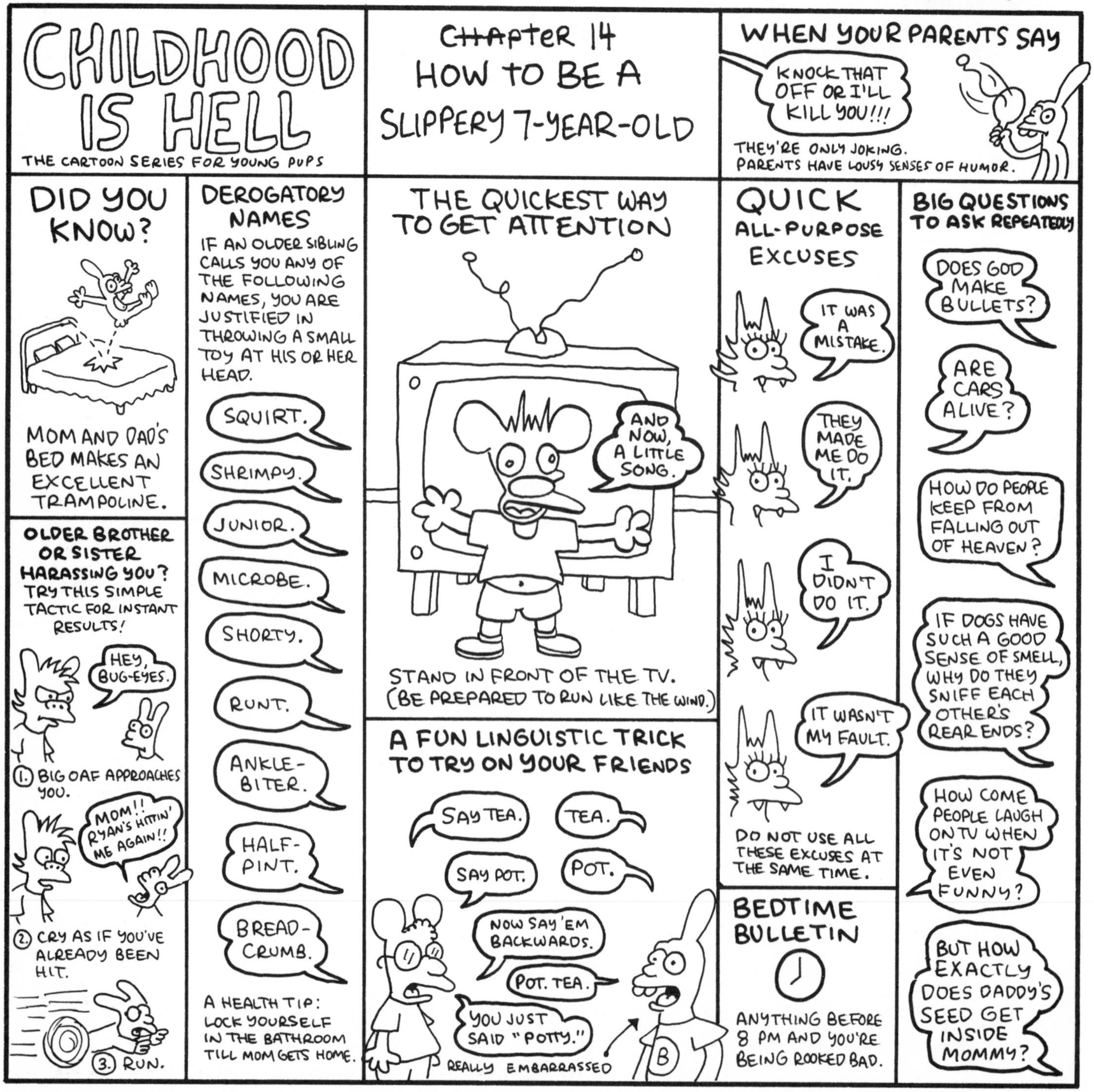
CHILDHOOD IS HELL
THE CARTOON SERIES FOR YOUNG PUPS
CHAPTER 14
HOW TO BE A SLIPPERY 7-YEAR-OLD
WHEN YOUR PARENTS SAY
KNOCK THAT OFF OR I'LL KILL YOU!!!
THEY'RE ONLY JOKING. PARENTS HAVE LOUSY SENSES OF HUMOR.
DID YOU KNOW?
MOM AND DAD'S BED MAKES AN EXCELLENT TRAMPOLINE.
OLDER BROTHER OR SISTER HARASSING YOU? TRY THIS SIMPLE TACTIC FOR INSTANT RESULTS!
HEY, BUG-EYES.
1. BIG OAF APPROACHES YOU.
MOM!! RYAN'S HITTIN' ME AGAIN!!
2. CRY AS IF YOU'VE ALREADY BEEN HIT.
3. RUN.
DEROGATORY NAMES
IF AN OLDER SIBLING CALLS YOU ANY OF THE FOLLOWING NAMES, YOU ARE JUSTIFIED IN THROWING A SMALL TOY AT HIS OR HER HEAD.
SQUIRT.
SHRIMPY.
JUNIOR.
MICROBE.
SHORTY.
RUNT.
ANKLE-BITER.
HALF-PINT.
BREAD-CRUMB.
A HEALTH TIP: LOCK YOURSELF IN THE BATHROOM TILL MOM GETS HOME.
THE QUICKEST WAY TO GET ATTENTION
AND NOW, A LITTLE SONG.
STAND IN FRONT OF THE TV. (BE PREPARED TO RUN LIKE THE WIND.)
A FUN LINGUISTIC TRICK TO TRY ON YOUR FRIENDS
SAY TEA.
TEA.
SAY POT.
POT.
NOW SAY 'EM BACKWARDS.
POT. TEA.
YOU JUST SAID "POTTY."
REALLY EMBARRASSED
QUICK ALL-PURPOSE EXCUSES
IT WAS A MISTAKE.
THEY MADE ME DO IT.
I DIDN'T DO IT.
IT WASN'T MY FAULT.
DO NOT USE ALL THESE EXCUSES AT THE SAME TIME.
BEDTIME BULLETIN
ANYTHING BEFORE 8 PM AND YOU'RE BEING ROOKED BAD.
BIG QUESTIONS TO ASK REPEATEDLY
DOES GOD MAKE BULLETS?
ARE CARS ALIVE?
HOW DO PEOPLE KEEP FROM FALLING OUT OF HEAVEN?
IF DOGS HAVE SUCH A GOOD SENSE OF SMELL, WHY DO THEY SNIFF EACH OTHER'S REAR ENDS?
HOW COME PEOPLE LAUGH ON TV WHEN IT'S NOT EVEN FUNNY?
BUT HOW EXACTLY DOES DADDY'S SEED GET INSIDE MOMMY?

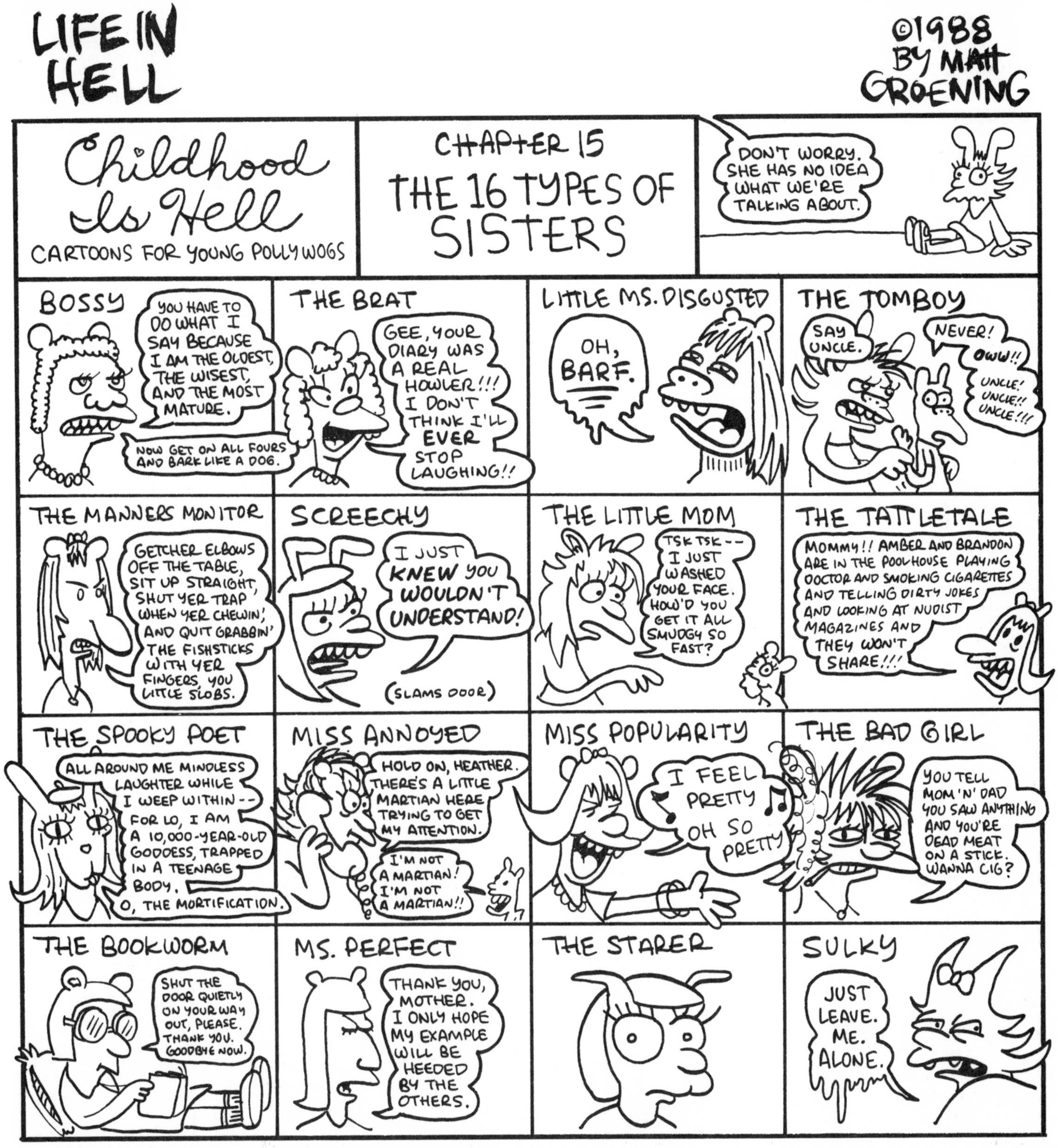

LIFE IN HELL
©1988 BY MATT GROENING
Childhood Is Hell
CARTOONS FOR YOUNG POLLYWOGS
CHAPTER 15
THE 16 TYPES OF SISTERS
DON'T WORRY. SHE HAS NO IDEA WHAT WE'RE TALKING ABOUT.
BOSSY
YOU HAVE TO DO WHAT I SAY BECAUSE I AM THE OLDEST, THE WISEST, AND THE MOST MATURE.
NOW GET ON ALL FOURS AND BARK LIKE A DOG.
THE BRAT
GEE, YOUR DIARY WAS A REAL HOWLER!!! I DON'T THINK I'LL EVER STOP LAUGHING!!
LITTLE MS. DISGUSTED
OH, BARF.
THE TOMBOY
SAY UNCLE.
NEVER!
OWW!!
UNCLE! UNCLE!! UNCLE!!!
THE MANNERS MONITOR
GETCHER ELBOWS OFF THE TABLE, SIT UP STRAIGHT, SHUT YER TRAP WHEN YER CHEWIN', AND QUIT GRABBIN' THE FISHSTICKS WITH YER FINGERS, YOU LITTLE SLOBS.
SCREECHY
I JUST KNEW YOU WOULDN'T UNDERSTAND!
(SLAMS DOOR)
THE LITTLE MOM
TSK TSK -- I JUST WASHED YOUR FACE. HOW'D YOU GET IT ALL SMUDGY SO FAST?
THE TATTLETALE
MOMMY!! AMBER AND BRANDON ARE IN THE POOLHOUSE PLAYING DOCTOR AND SMOKING CIGARETTES AND TELLING DIRTY JOKES AND LOOKING AT NUDIST MAGAZINES AND THEY WON'T SHARE!!!
THE SPOOKY POET
ALL AROUND ME MINDLESS LAUGHTER WHILE I WEEP WITHIN -- FOR LO, I AM A 10,000-YEAR-OLD GODDESS, TRAPPED IN A TEENAGE BODY.
O, THE MORTIFICATION.
MISS ANNOYED
HOLD ON, HEATHER. THERE'S A LITTLE MARTIAN HERE TRYING TO GET MY ATTENTION.
I'M NOT A MARTIAN! I'M NOT A MARTIAN!!
MISS POPULARITY
I FEEL PRETTY OH SO PRETTY
THE BAD GIRL
YOU TELL MOM 'N' DAD YOU SAW ANYTHING AND YOU'RE DEAD MEAT ON A STICK. WANNA CIG?
THE BOOKWORM
SHUT THE DOOR QUIETLY ON YOUR WAY OUT, PLEASE. THANK YOU. GOODBYE NOW.
MS. PERFECT
THANK YOU, MOTHER. I ONLY HOPE MY EXAMPLE WILL BE HEEDED BY THE OTHERS.
THE STARER
SULKY
JUST LEAVE. ME. ALONE.

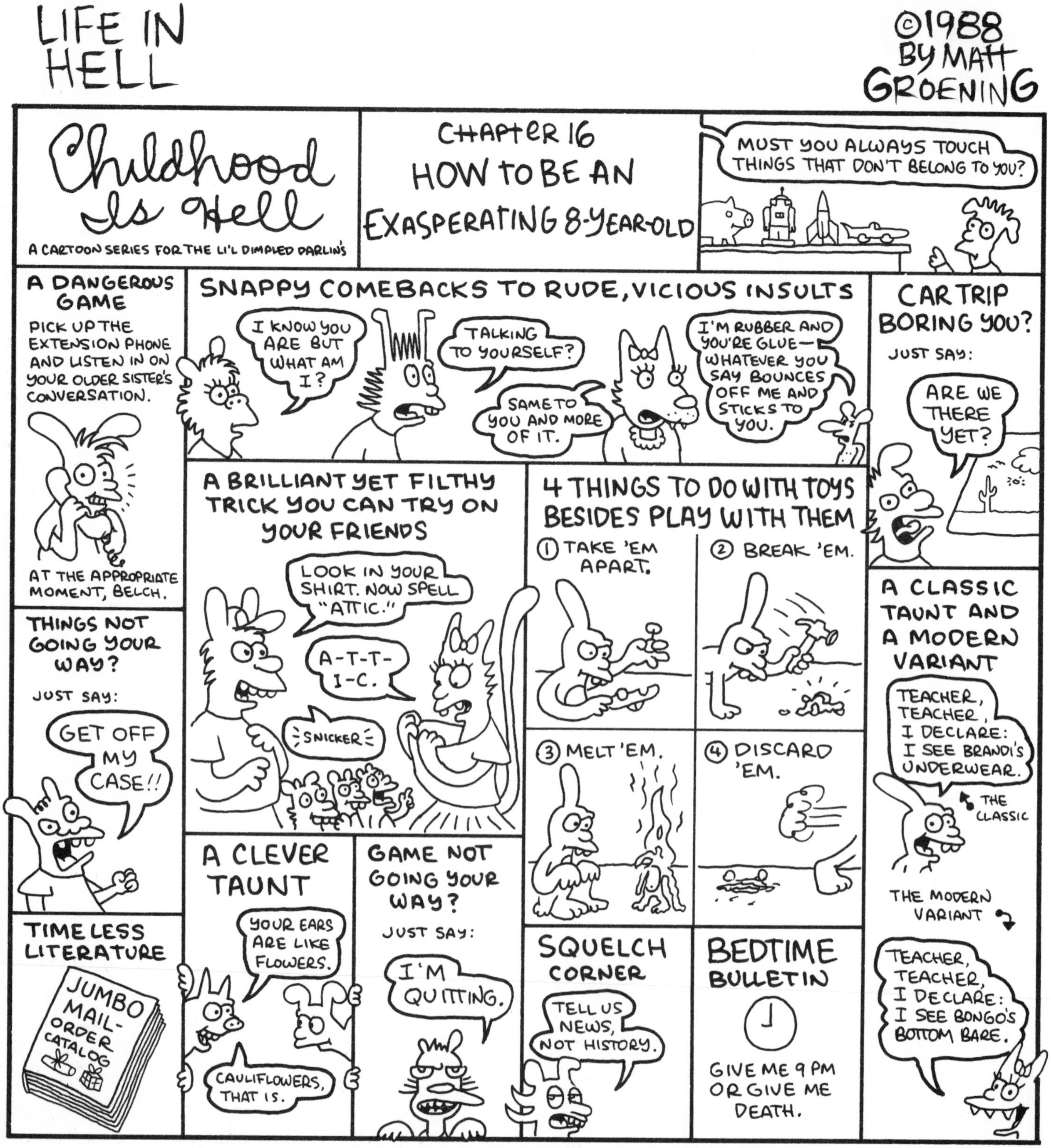
LIFE IN HELL
©1988 BY MATT GROENING
Childhood Is Hell
A CARTOON SERIES FOR THE LI'L DIMPLED DARLIN'S
CHAPTER 16
HOW TO BE AN EXASPERATING 8-YEAR-OLD
MUST YOU ALWAYS TOUCH THINGS THAT DON'T BELONG TO YOU?
A DANGEROUS GAME
PICK UP THE EXTENSION PHONE AND LISTEN IN ON YOUR OLDER SISTER'S CONVERSATION.
AT THE APPROPRIATE MOMENT, BELCH.
SNAPPY COMEBACKS TO RUDE, VICIOUS INSULTS
I KNOW YOU ARE BUT WHAT AM I?
TALKING TO YOURSELF?
SAME TO YOU AND MORE OF IT.
I'M RUBBER AND YOU'RE GLUE— WHATEVER YOU SAY BOUNCES OFF ME AND STICKS TO YOU.
CAR TRIP BORING YOU?
JUST SAY:
ARE WE THERE YET?
THINGS NOT GOING YOUR WAY?
JUST SAY:
GET OFF MY CASE!!
A BRILLIANT YET FILTHY TRICK YOU CAN TRY ON YOUR FRIENDS
LOOK IN YOUR SHIRT. NOW SPELL "ATTIC."
A-T-T-I-C.
SNICKER
4 THINGS TO DO WITH TOYS BESIDES PLAY WITH THEM
① TAKE 'EM APART.
② BREAK 'EM.
③ MELT 'EM.
④ DISCARD 'EM.
A CLASSIC TAUNT AND A MODERN VARIANT
TEACHER, TEACHER, I DECLARE: I SEE BRANDI'S UNDERWEAR.
THE CLASSIC
THE MODERN VARIANT
TEACHER, TEACHER, I DECLARE: I SEE BONGO'S BOTTOM BARE.
TIMELESS LITERATURE
JUMBO MAIL-ORDER CATALOG
A CLEVER TAUNT
YOUR EARS ARE LIKE FLOWERS.
CAULIFLOWERS, THAT IS.
GAME NOT GOING YOUR WAY?
JUST SAY:
I'M QUITTING.
SQUELCH CORNER
TELL US NEWS, NOT HISTORY.
BEDTIME BULLETIN
GIVE ME 9 PM OR GIVE ME DEATH.

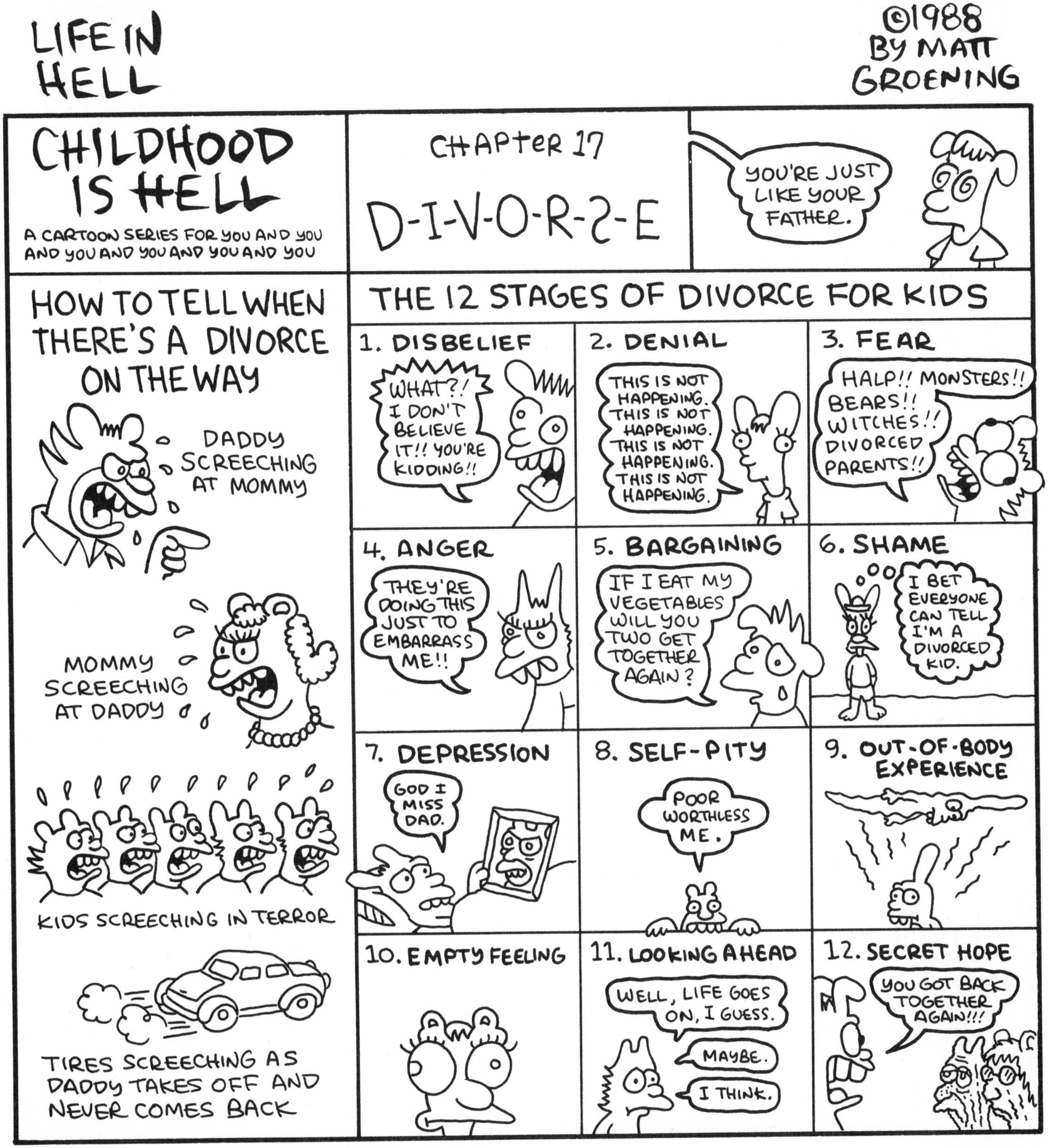

LIFE IN HELL
©1988 BY MATT GROENING
CHILDHOOD IS HELL
A CARTOON SERIES FOR YOU AND YOU AND YOU AND YOU AND YOU AND YOU
CHAPTER 17
D-I-V-O-R-S-E
YOU'RE JUST LIKE YOUR FATHER.
HOW TO TELL WHEN THERE'S A DIVORCE ON THE WAY
DADDY SCREECHING AT MOMMY
MOMMY SCREECHING AT DADDY
KIDS SCREECHING IN TERROR
TIRES SCREECHING AS DADDY TAKES OFF AND NEVER COMES BACK
THE 12 STAGES OF DIVORCE FOR KIDS
1. DISBELIEF
WHAT?! I DON'T BELIEVE IT!! YOU'RE KIDDING!!
2. DENIAL
THIS IS NOT HAPPENING. THIS IS NOT HAPPENING. THIS IS NOT HAPPENING. THIS IS NOT HAPPENING.
3. FEAR
HALP!! MONSTERS!! BEARS!! WITCHES!! DIVORCED PARENTS!!
4. ANGER
THEY'RE DOING THIS JUST TO EMBARRASS ME!!
5. BARGAINING
IF I EAT MY VEGETABLES WILL YOU TWO GET TOGETHER AGAIN?
6. SHAME
I BET EVERYONE CAN TELL I'M A DIVORCED KID.
7. DEPRESSION
GOD I MISS DAD.
8. SELF-PITY
POOR WORTHLESS ME.
9. OUT-OF-BODY EXPERIENCE
10. EMPTY FEELING
11. LOOKING AHEAD
WELL, LIFE GOES ON, I GUESS.
MAYBE.
I THINK.
12. SECRET HOPE
YOU GOT BACK TOGETHER AGAIN!!!

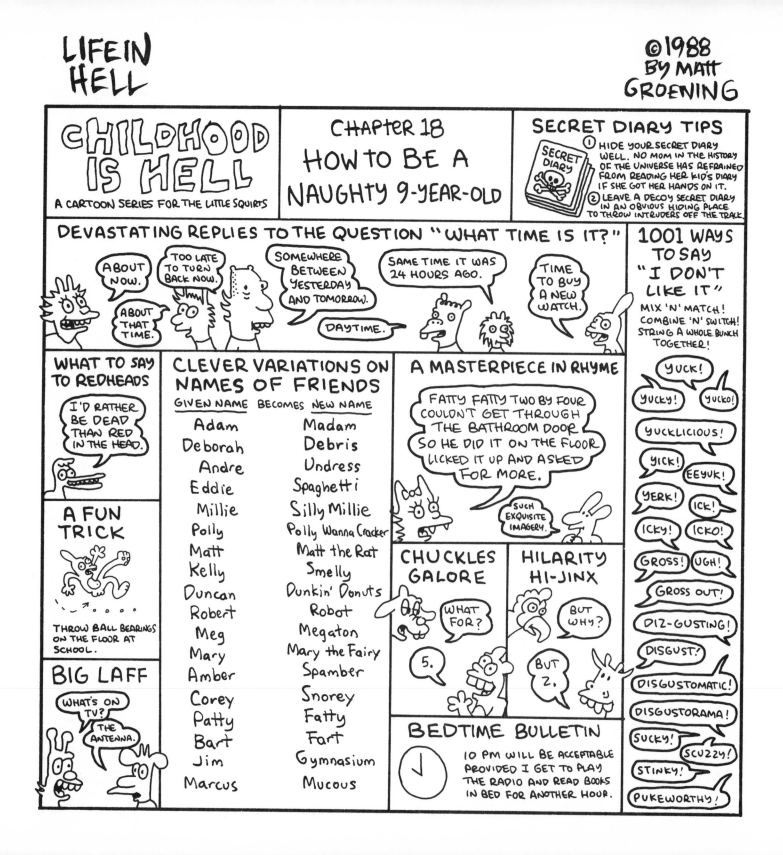

LIFE IN HELL

©1988 By Matt Groening

CHILDHOOD IS HELL
A CARTOON SERIES FOR THE LITTLE SQUIRTS

CHAPTER 18
HOW TO BE A NAUGHTY 9-YEAR-OLD

SECRET DIARY TIPS
SECRET DIARY

1. HIDE YOUR SECRET DIARY WELL. NO MOM IN THE HISTORY OF THE UNIVERSE HAS REFRAINED FROM READING HER KID'S DIARY IF SHE GOT HER HANDS ON IT.
2. LEAVE A DECOY SECRET DIARY IN AN OBVIOUS HIDING PLACE TO THROW INTRUDERS OFF THE TRACK.

DEVASTATING REPLIES TO THE QUESTION "WHAT TIME IS IT?"

- ABOUT NOW.
- ABOUT THAT TIME.
- TOO LATE TO TURN BACK NOW.
- SOMEWHERE BETWEEN YESTERDAY AND TOMORROW.
- DAYTIME.
- SAME TIME IT WAS 24 HOURS AGO.
- TIME TO BUY A NEW WATCH.

1001 WAYS TO SAY "I DON'T LIKE IT"
MIX 'N' MATCH! COMBINE 'N' SWITCH! STRING A WHOLE BUNCH TOGETHER!

- YUCK!
- YUCKY!
- YUCKO!
- YUCKLICIOUS!
- YICK!
- EEYUK!
- YERK!
- ICK!
- ICKY!
- ICKO!
- GROSS!
- UGH!
- GROSS OUT!
- DIZ-GUSTING!
- DISGUST!
- DISGUSTOMATIC!
- DISGUSTORAMA!
- SUCKY!
- SCUZZY!
- STINKY!
- PUKEWORTHY!

WHAT TO SAY TO REDHEADS
I'D RATHER BE DEAD THAN RED IN THE HEAD.

A FUN TRICK
THROW BALL BEARINGS ON THE FLOOR AT SCHOOL.

BIG LAFF
WHAT'S ON TV? THE ANTENNA.

CLEVER VARIATIONS ON NAMES OF FRIENDS

GIVEN NAME	BECOMES	NEW NAME
Adam		Madam
Deborah		Debris
Andre		Undress
Eddie		Spaghetti
Millie		Silly Millie
Polly		Polly Wanna Cracker
Matt		Matt the Rat
Kelly		Smelly
Duncan		Dunkin' Donuts
Robert		Robot
Meg		Megaton
Mary		Mary the Fairy
Amber		Spamber
Corey		Snorey
Patty		Fatty
Bart		Fart
Jim		Gymnasium
Marcus		Mucous

A MASTERPIECE IN RHYME
FATTY FATTY TWO BY FOUR COULDN'T GET THROUGH THE BATHROOM DOOR SO HE DID IT ON THE FLOOR LICKED IT UP AND ASKED FOR MORE.

SUCH EXQUISITE IMAGERY.

CHUCKLES GALORE
WHAT FOR?
5.

HILARITY HI-JINX
BUT WHY?
BUT 2.

BEDTIME BULLETIN
10 PM WILL BE ACCEPTABLE PROVIDED I GET TO PLAY THE RADIO AND READ BOOKS IN BED FOR ANOTHER HOUR.

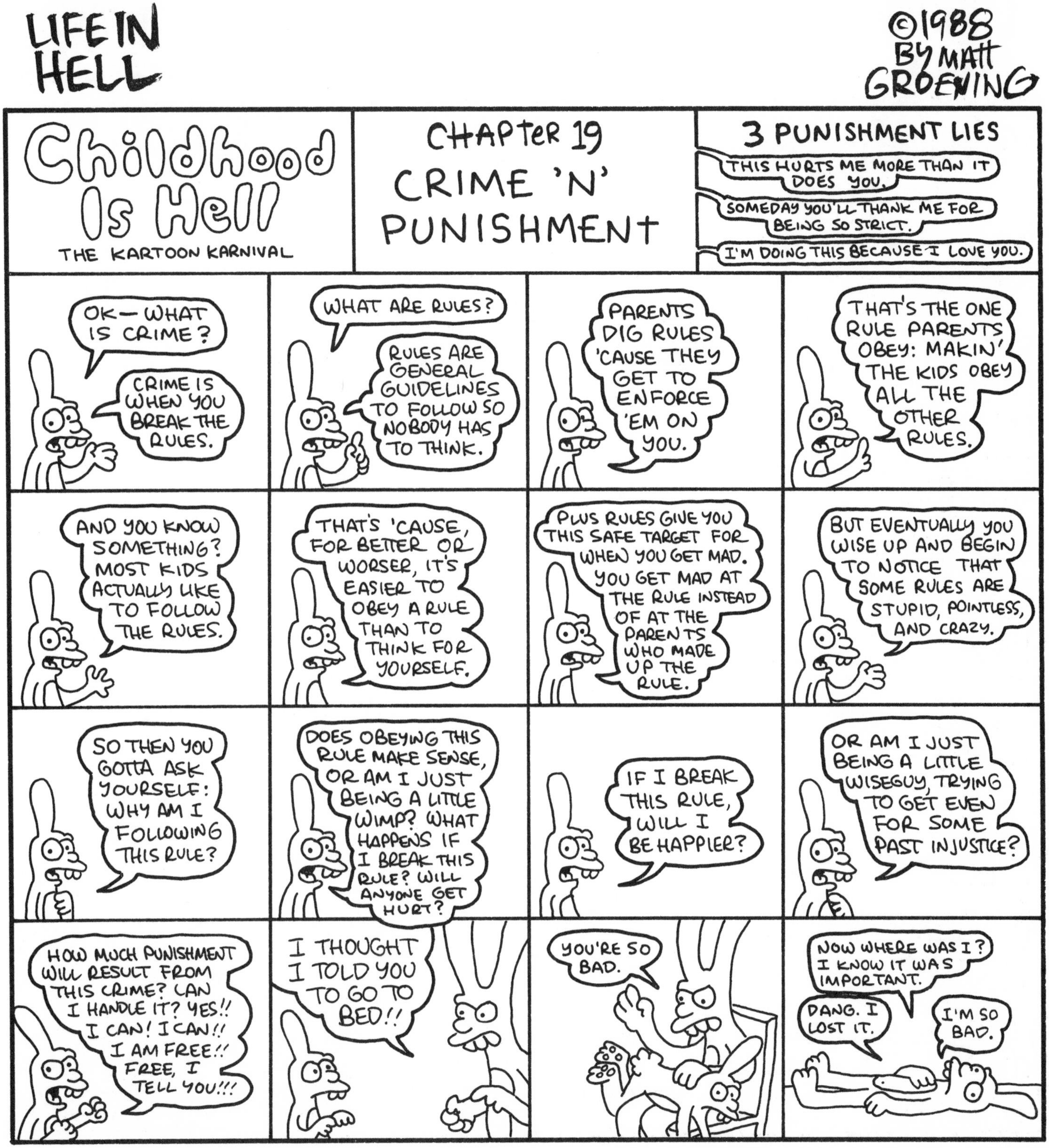
LIFE IN HELL
©1988 BY MATT GROENING
Childhood Is Hell
THE KARTOON KARNIVAL
CHAPTER 19
CRIME 'N' PUNISHMENT
3 PUNISHMENT LIES
THIS HURTS ME MORE THAN IT DOES YOU.
SOMEDAY YOU'LL THANK ME FOR BEING SO STRICT.
I'M DOING THIS BECAUSE I LOVE YOU.
OK— WHAT IS CRIME?
CRIME IS WHEN YOU BREAK THE RULES.
WHAT ARE RULES?
RULES ARE GENERAL GUIDELINES TO FOLLOW SO NOBODY HAS TO THINK.
PARENTS DIG RULES 'CAUSE THEY GET TO ENFORCE 'EM ON YOU.
THAT'S THE ONE RULE PARENTS OBEY: MAKIN' THE KIDS OBEY ALL THE OTHER RULES.
AND YOU KNOW SOMETHING? MOST KIDS ACTUALLY LIKE TO FOLLOW THE RULES.
THAT'S 'CAUSE, FOR BETTER OR WORSER, IT'S EASIER TO OBEY A RULE THAN TO THINK FOR YOURSELF.
PLUS RULES GIVE YOU THIS SAFE TARGET FOR WHEN YOU GET MAD. YOU GET MAD AT THE RULE INSTEAD OF AT THE PARENTS WHO MADE UP THE RULE.
BUT EVENTUALLY YOU WISE UP AND BEGIN TO NOTICE THAT SOME RULES ARE STUPID, POINTLESS, AND CRAZY.
SO THEN YOU GOTTA ASK YOURSELF: WHY AM I FOLLOWING THIS RULE?
DOES OBEYING THIS RULE MAKE SENSE, OR AM I JUST BEING A LITTLE WIMP? WHAT HAPPENS IF I BREAK THIS RULE? WILL ANYONE GET HURT?
IF I BREAK THIS RULE, WILL I BE HAPPIER?
OR AM I JUST BEING A LITTLE WISEGUY, TRYING TO GET EVEN FOR SOME PAST INJUSTICE?
HOW MUCH PUNISHMENT WILL RESULT FROM THIS CRIME? CAN I HANDLE IT? YES!! I CAN! I CAN!! I AM FREE!! FREE, I TELL YOU!!!
I THOUGHT I TOLD YOU TO GO TO BED!!
YOU'RE SO BAD.
NOW WHERE WAS I? I KNOW IT WAS IMPORTANT.
DANG. I LOST IT.
I'M SO BAD.

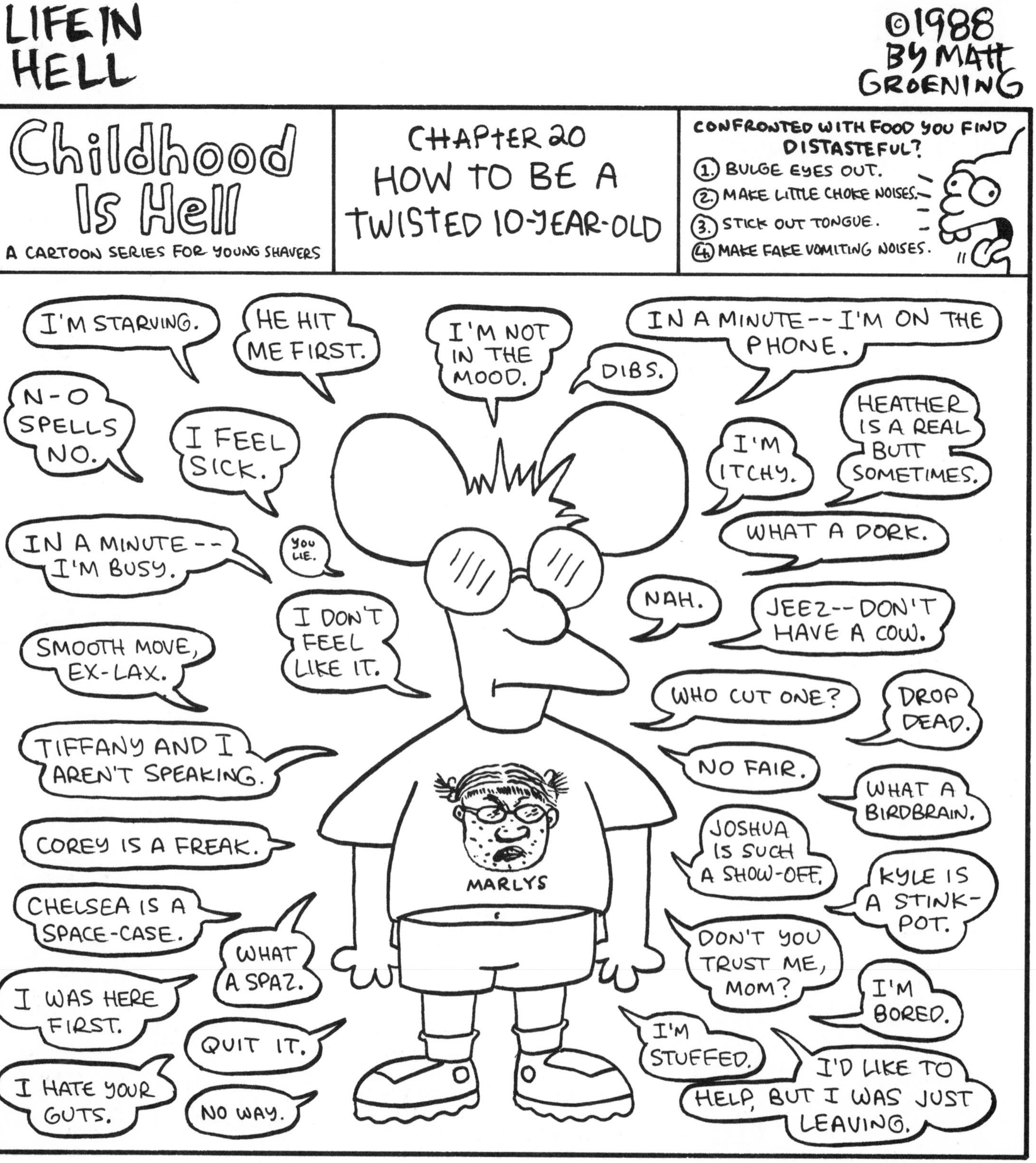
LIFE IN HELL
©1988 BY MATT GROENING
Childhood Is Hell
A CARTOON SERIES FOR YOUNG SHAVERS
CHAPTER 20
HOW TO BE A TWISTED 10-YEAR-OLD
CONFRONTED WITH FOOD YOU FIND DISTASTEFUL?
1. BULGE EYES OUT.
2. MAKE LITTLE CHOKE NOISES.
3. STICK OUT TONGUE.
4. MAKE FAKE VOMITING NOISES.
I'M STARVING.
HE HIT ME FIRST.
I'M NOT IN THE MOOD.
DIBS.
IN A MINUTE -- I'M ON THE PHONE.
N-O SPELLS NO.
I FEEL SICK.
I'M ITCHY.
HEATHER IS A REAL BUTT SOMETIMES.
IN A MINUTE -- I'M BUSY.
YOU LIE.
WHAT A DORK.
NAH.
JEEZ -- DON'T HAVE A COW.
I DON'T FEEL LIKE IT.
SMOOTH MOVE, EX-LAX.
WHO CUT ONE?
DROP DEAD.
TIFFANY AND I AREN'T SPEAKING.
NO FAIR.
WHAT A BIRDBRAIN.
MARLYS
COREY IS A FREAK.
JOSHUA IS SUCH A SHOW-OFF.
KYLE IS A STINK-POT.
CHELSEA IS A SPACE-CASE.
WHAT A SPAZ.
DON'T YOU TRUST ME, MOM?
I WAS HERE FIRST.
I'M BORED.
QUIT IT.
I'M STUFFED.
I HATE YOUR GUTS.
NO WAY.
I'D LIKE TO HELP, BUT I WAS JUST LEAVING.

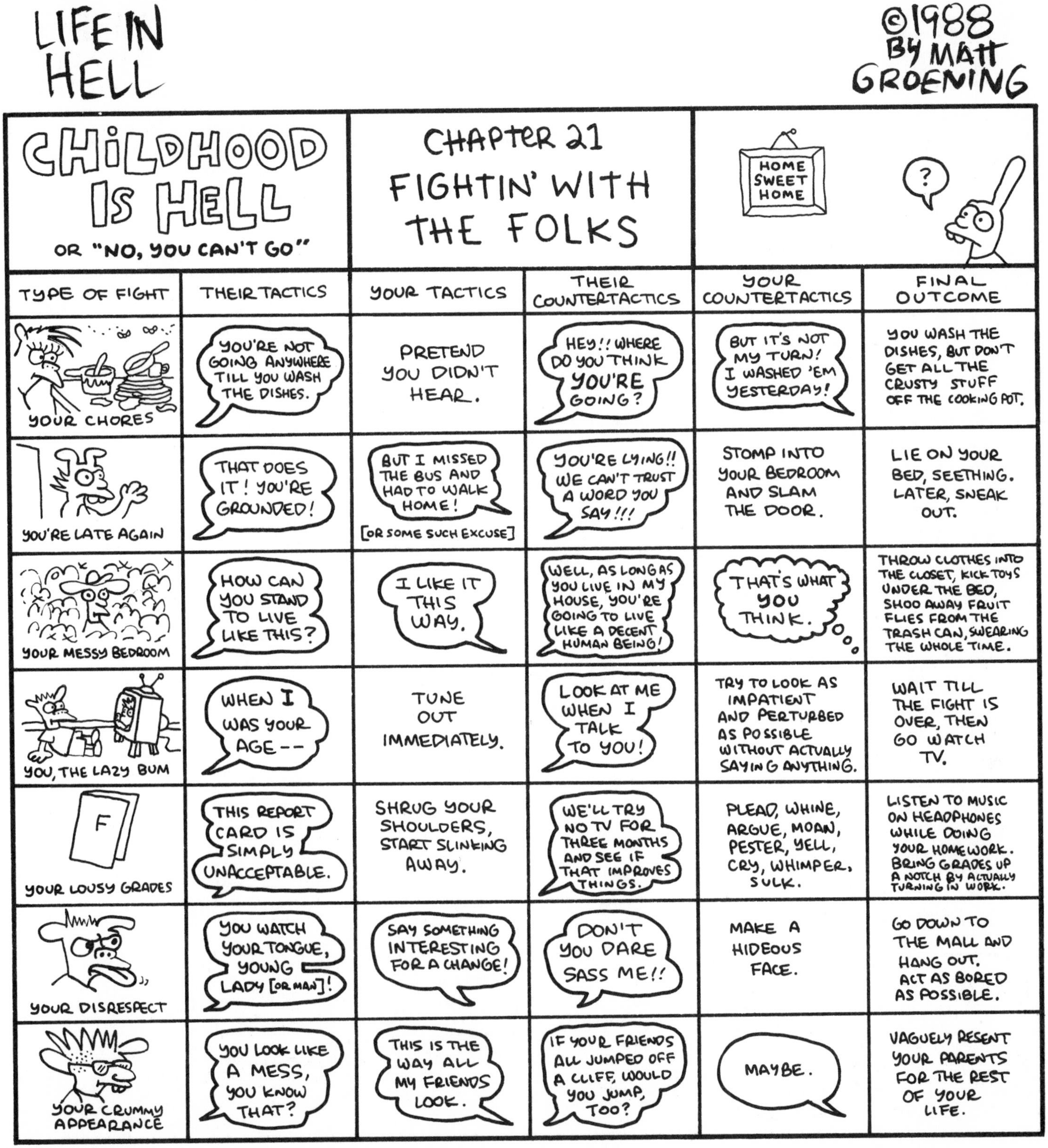

LIFE IN HELL
©1988 BY MATT GROENING
CHILDHOOD IS HELL
OR "NO, YOU CAN'T GO"
CHAPTER 21
FIGHTIN' WITH THE FOLKS
HOME SWEET HOME
?
TYPE OF FIGHT
THEIR TACTICS
YOUR TACTICS
THEIR COUNTERTACTICS
YOUR COUNTERTACTICS
FINAL OUTCOME
YOUR CHORES
YOU'RE NOT GOING ANYWHERE TILL YOU WASH THE DISHES.
PRETEND YOU DIDN'T HEAR.
HEY!! WHERE DO YOU THINK YOU'RE GOING?
BUT IT'S NOT MY TURN! I WASHED 'EM YESTERDAY!
YOU WASH THE DISHES, BUT DON'T GET ALL THE CRUSTY STUFF OFF THE COOKING POT.
YOU'RE LATE AGAIN
THAT DOES IT! YOU'RE GROUNDED!
BUT I MISSED THE BUS AND HAD TO WALK HOME!
[OR SOME SUCH EXCUSE]
YOU'RE LYING!! WE CAN'T TRUST A WORD YOU SAY!!!
STOMP INTO YOUR BEDROOM AND SLAM THE DOOR.
LIE ON YOUR BED, SEETHING. LATER, SNEAK OUT.
YOUR MESSY BEDROOM
HOW CAN YOU STAND TO LIVE LIKE THIS?
I LIKE IT THIS WAY.
WELL, AS LONG AS YOU LIVE IN MY HOUSE, YOU'RE GOING TO LIVE LIKE A DECENT HUMAN BEING!
THAT'S WHAT YOU THINK.
THROW CLOTHES INTO THE CLOSET, KICK TOYS UNDER THE BED, SHOO AWAY FRUIT FLIES FROM THE TRASH CAN, SWEARING THE WHOLE TIME.
YOU, THE LAZY BUM
WHEN I WAS YOUR AGE--
TUNE OUT IMMEDIATELY.
LOOK AT ME WHEN I TALK TO YOU!
TRY TO LOOK AS IMPATIENT AND PERTURBED AS POSSIBLE WITHOUT ACTUALLY SAYING ANYTHING.
WAIT TILL THE FIGHT IS OVER, THEN GO WATCH TV.
F
YOUR LOUSY GRADES
THIS REPORT CARD IS SIMPLY UNACCEPTABLE.
SHRUG YOUR SHOULDERS, START SLINKING AWAY.
WE'LL TRY NO TV FOR THREE MONTHS AND SEE IF THAT IMPROVES THINGS.
PLEAD, WHINE, ARGUE, MOAN, PESTER, YELL, CRY, WHIMPER, SULK.
LISTEN TO MUSIC ON HEADPHONES WHILE DOING YOUR HOMEWORK. BRING GRADES UP A NOTCH BY ACTUALLY TURNING IN WORK.
YOUR DISRESPECT
YOU WATCH YOUR TONGUE, YOUNG LADY [OR MAN]!
SAY SOMETHING INTERESTING FOR A CHANGE!
DON'T YOU DARE SASS ME!!
MAKE A HIDEOUS FACE.
GO DOWN TO THE MALL AND HANG OUT. ACT AS BORED AS POSSIBLE.
YOUR CRUMMY APPEARANCE
YOU LOOK LIKE A MESS, YOU KNOW THAT?
THIS IS THE WAY ALL MY FRIENDS LOOK.
IF YOUR FRIENDS ALL JUMPED OFF A CLIFF, WOULD YOU JUMP, TOO?
MAYBE.
VAGUELY RESENT YOUR PARENTS FOR THE REST OF YOUR LIFE.

LIFE IN HELL

©1988 BY MATT GROENING

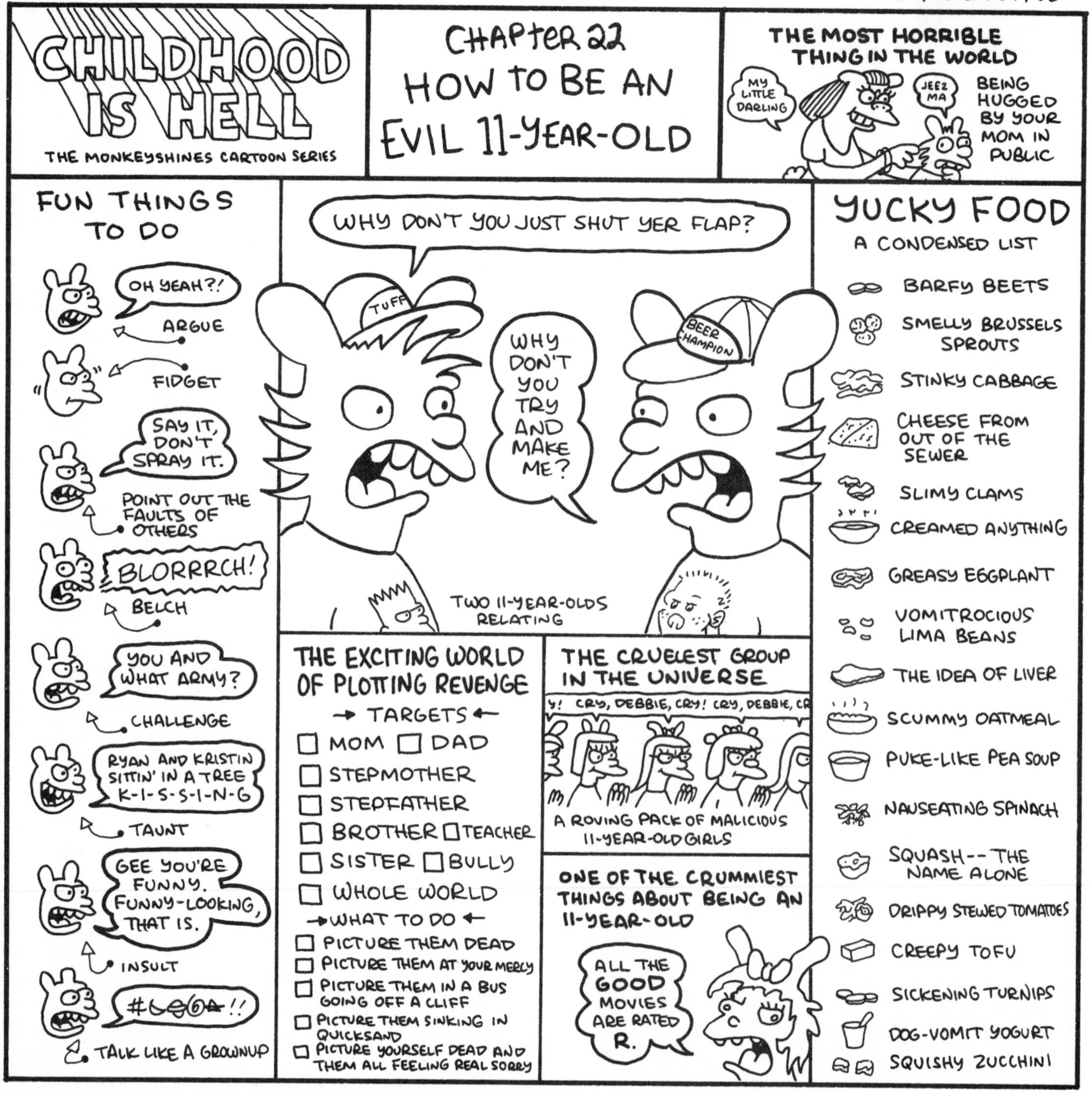
CHILDHOOD IS HELL
THE MONKEYSHINES CARTOON SERIES
CHAPTER 22
HOW TO BE AN EVIL 11-YEAR-OLD
THE MOST HORRIBLE THING IN THE WORLD
MY LITTLE DARLING
JEEZ MA
BEING HUGGED BY YOUR MOM IN PUBLIC
FUN THINGS TO DO
OH YEAH?!
ARGUE
FIDGET
SAY IT, DON'T SPRAY IT.
POINT OUT THE FAULTS OF OTHERS
BLORRRCH!
BELCH
YOU AND WHAT ARMY?
CHALLENGE
RYAN AND KRISTIN SITTIN' IN A TREE K-I-S-S-I-N-G
TAUNT
GEE YOU'RE FUNNY. FUNNY-LOOKING, THAT IS.
INSULT
TALK LIKE A GROWNUP
WHY DON'T YOU JUST SHUT YER FLAP?
TUFF
BEER CHAMPION
WHY DON'T YOU TRY AND MAKE ME?
TWO 11-YEAR-OLDS RELATING
YUCKY FOOD
A CONDENSED LIST
BARFY BEETS
SMELLY BRUSSELS SPROUTS
STINKY CABBAGE
CHEESE FROM OUT OF THE SEWER
SLIMY CLAMS
CREAMED ANYTHING
GREASY EGGPLANT
VOMITROCIOUS LIMA BEANS
THE IDEA OF LIVER
SCUMMY OATMEAL
PUKE-LIKE PEA SOUP
NAUSEATING SPINACH
SQUASH -- THE NAME ALONE
DRIPPY STEWED TOMATOES
CREEPY TOFU
SICKENING TURNIPS
DOG-VOMIT YOGURT
SQUISHY ZUCCHINI
THE EXCITING WORLD OF PLOTTING REVENGE
→ TARGETS ←
☐ MOM ☐ DAD
☐ STEPMOTHER
☐ STEPFATHER
☐ BROTHER ☐ TEACHER
☐ SISTER ☐ BULLY
☐ WHOLE WORLD
→ WHAT TO DO ←
☐ PICTURE THEM DEAD
☐ PICTURE THEM AT YOUR MERCY
☐ PICTURE THEM IN A BUS GOING OFF A CLIFF
☐ PICTURE THEM SINKING IN QUICKSAND
☐ PICTURE YOURSELF DEAD AND THEM ALL FEELING REAL SORRY
THE CRUELEST GROUP IN THE UNIVERSE
Y! CRY, DEBBIE, CRY! CRY, DEBBIE, CR
A ROVING PACK OF MALICIOUS 11-YEAR-OLD GIRLS
ONE OF THE CRUMMIEST THINGS ABOUT BEING AN 11-YEAR-OLD
ALL THE GOOD MOVIES ARE RATED R.

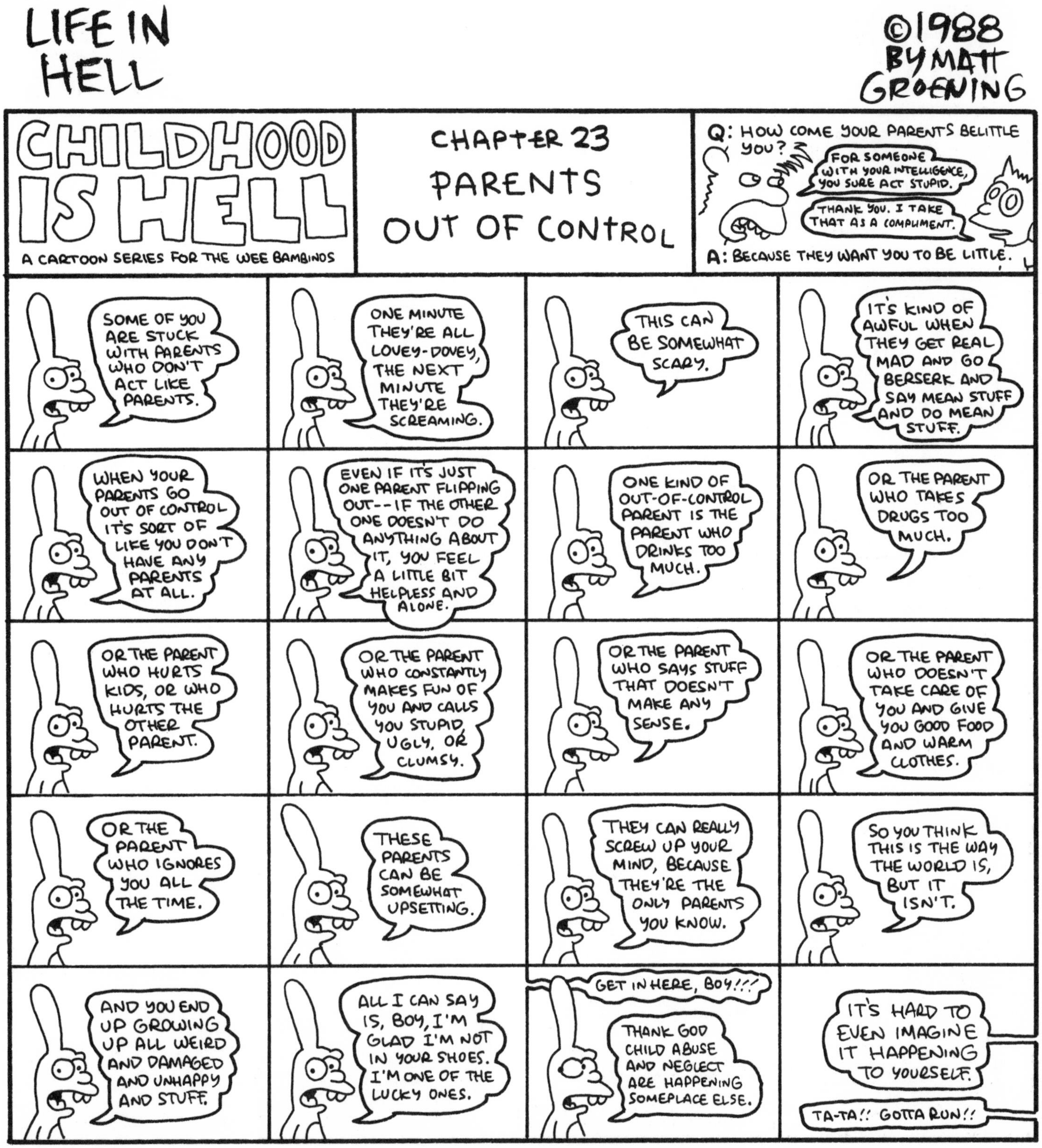
LIFE IN HELL
©1988 BY MATT GROENING
CHILDHOOD IS HELL
A CARTOON SERIES FOR THE WEE BAMBINOS
CHAPTER 23
PARENTS OUT OF CONTROL
Q: HOW COME YOUR PARENTS BELITTLE YOU?
FOR SOMEONE WITH YOUR INTELLIGENCE, YOU SURE ACT STUPID.
THANK YOU. I TAKE THAT AS A COMPLIMENT.
A: BECAUSE THEY WANT YOU TO BE LITTLE.
SOME OF YOU ARE STUCK WITH PARENTS WHO DON'T ACT LIKE PARENTS.
ONE MINUTE THEY'RE ALL LOVEY-DOVEY, THE NEXT MINUTE THEY'RE SCREAMING.
THIS CAN BE SOMEWHAT SCARY.
IT'S KIND OF AWFUL WHEN THEY GET REAL MAD AND GO BERSERK AND SAY MEAN STUFF AND DO MEAN STUFF.
WHEN YOUR PARENTS GO OUT OF CONTROL IT'S SORT OF LIKE YOU DON'T HAVE ANY PARENTS AT ALL.
EVEN IF IT'S JUST ONE PARENT FLIPPING OUT--IF THE OTHER ONE DOESN'T DO ANYTHING ABOUT IT, YOU FEEL A LITTLE BIT HELPLESS AND ALONE.
ONE KIND OF OUT-OF-CONTROL PARENT IS THE PARENT WHO DRINKS TOO MUCH.
OR THE PARENT WHO TAKES DRUGS TOO MUCH.
OR THE PARENT WHO HURTS KIDS, OR WHO HURTS THE OTHER PARENT.
OR THE PARENT WHO CONSTANTLY MAKES FUN OF YOU AND CALLS YOU STUPID, UGLY, OR CLUMSY.
OR THE PARENT WHO SAYS STUFF THAT DOESN'T MAKE ANY SENSE.
OR THE PARENT WHO DOESN'T TAKE CARE OF YOU AND GIVE YOU GOOD FOOD AND WARM CLOTHES.
OR THE PARENT WHO IGNORES YOU ALL THE TIME.
THESE PARENTS CAN BE SOMEWHAT UPSETTING.
THEY CAN REALLY SCREW UP YOUR MIND, BECAUSE THEY'RE THE ONLY PARENTS YOU KNOW.
SO YOU THINK THIS IS THE WAY THE WORLD IS, BUT IT ISN'T.
AND YOU END UP GROWING UP ALL WEIRD AND DAMAGED AND UNHAPPY AND STUFF.
ALL I CAN SAY IS, BOY, I'M GLAD I'M NOT IN YOUR SHOES. I'M ONE OF THE LUCKY ONES.
GET IN HERE, BOY!!!
THANK GOD CHILD ABUSE AND NEGLECT ARE HAPPENING SOMEPLACE ELSE.
IT'S HARD TO EVEN IMAGINE IT HAPPENING TO YOURSELF.
TA-TA!! GOTTA RUN!!

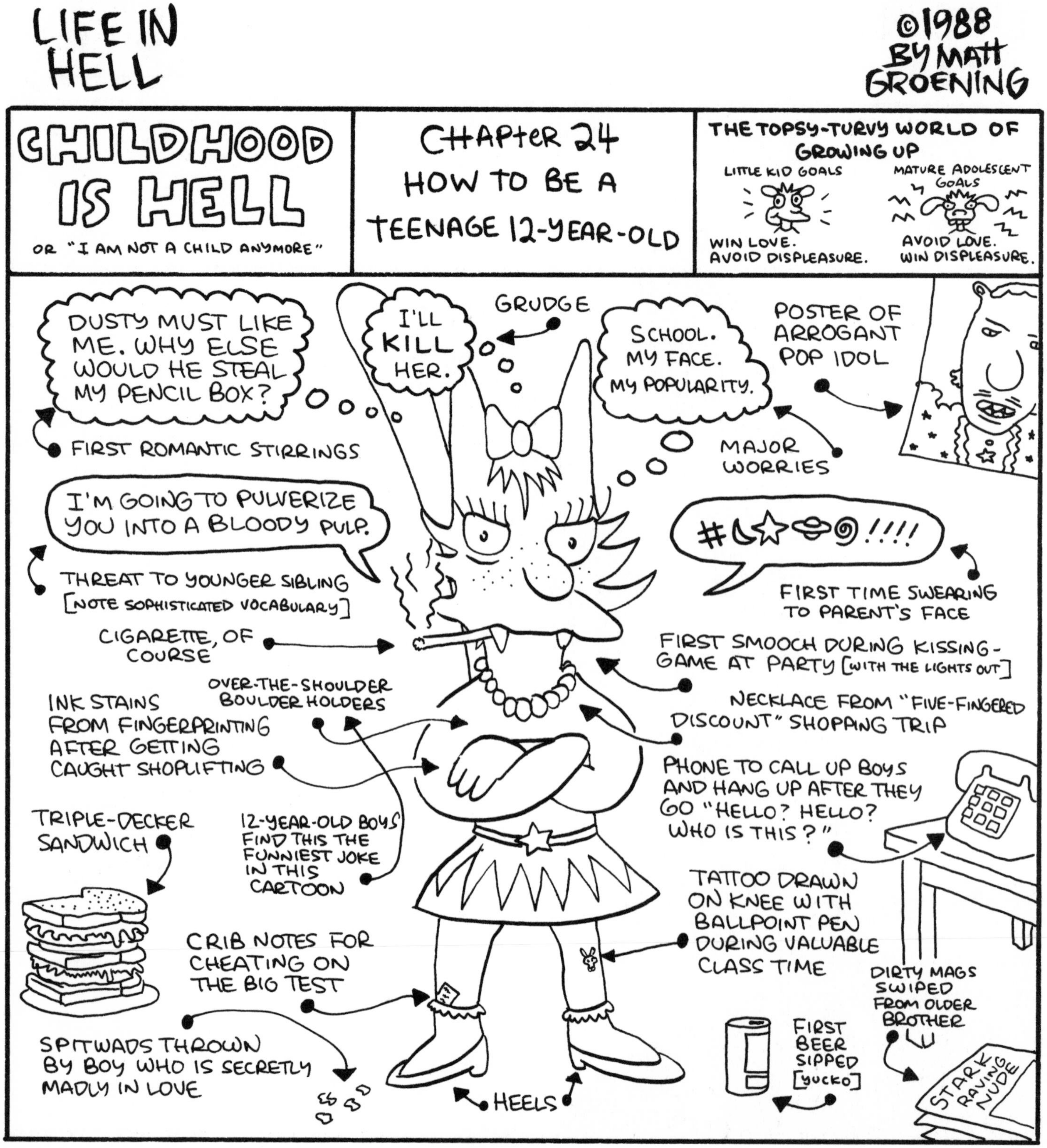

LIFE IN HELL
©1988 BY MATT GROENING
CHILDHOOD IS HELL
OR "I AM NOT A CHILD ANYMORE"
CHAPTER 24
HOW TO BE A TEENAGE 12-YEAR-OLD
THE TOPSY-TURVY WORLD OF GROWING UP
LITTLE KID GOALS
MATURE ADOLESCENT GOALS
WIN LOVE. AVOID DISPLEASURE.
AVOID LOVE. WIN DISPLEASURE.
DUSTY MUST LIKE ME. WHY ELSE WOULD HE STEAL MY PENCIL BOX?
I'LL KILL HER.
GRUDGE
SCHOOL. MY FACE. MY POPULARITY.
POSTER OF ARROGANT POP IDOL
FIRST ROMANTIC STIRRINGS
MAJOR WORRIES
I'M GOING TO PULVERIZE YOU INTO A BLOODY PULP.
#☾☆🪐◎!!!!
THREAT TO YOUNGER SIBLING [NOTE SOPHISTICATED VOCABULARY]
FIRST TIME SWEARING TO PARENT'S FACE
CIGARETTE, OF COURSE
FIRST SMOOCH DURING KISSING-GAME AT PARTY [WITH THE LIGHTS OUT]
OVER-THE-SHOULDER BOULDER HOLDERS
INK STAINS FROM FINGERPRINTING AFTER GETTING CAUGHT SHOPLIFTING
NECKLACE FROM "FIVE-FINGERED DISCOUNT" SHOPPING TRIP
PHONE TO CALL UP BOYS AND HANG UP AFTER THEY GO "HELLO? HELLO? WHO IS THIS?"
TRIPLE-DECKER SANDWICH
12-YEAR-OLD BOYS FIND THIS THE FUNNIEST JOKE IN THIS CARTOON
TATTOO DRAWN ON KNEE WITH BALLPOINT PEN DURING VALUABLE CLASS TIME
CRIB NOTES FOR CHEATING ON THE BIG TEST
DIRTY MAGS SWIPED FROM OLDER BROTHER
SPITWADS THROWN BY BOY WHO IS SECRETLY MADLY IN LOVE
FIRST BEER SIPPED [YUCKO]
HEELS
STARK RAVING NUDE

LIFE IN HELL

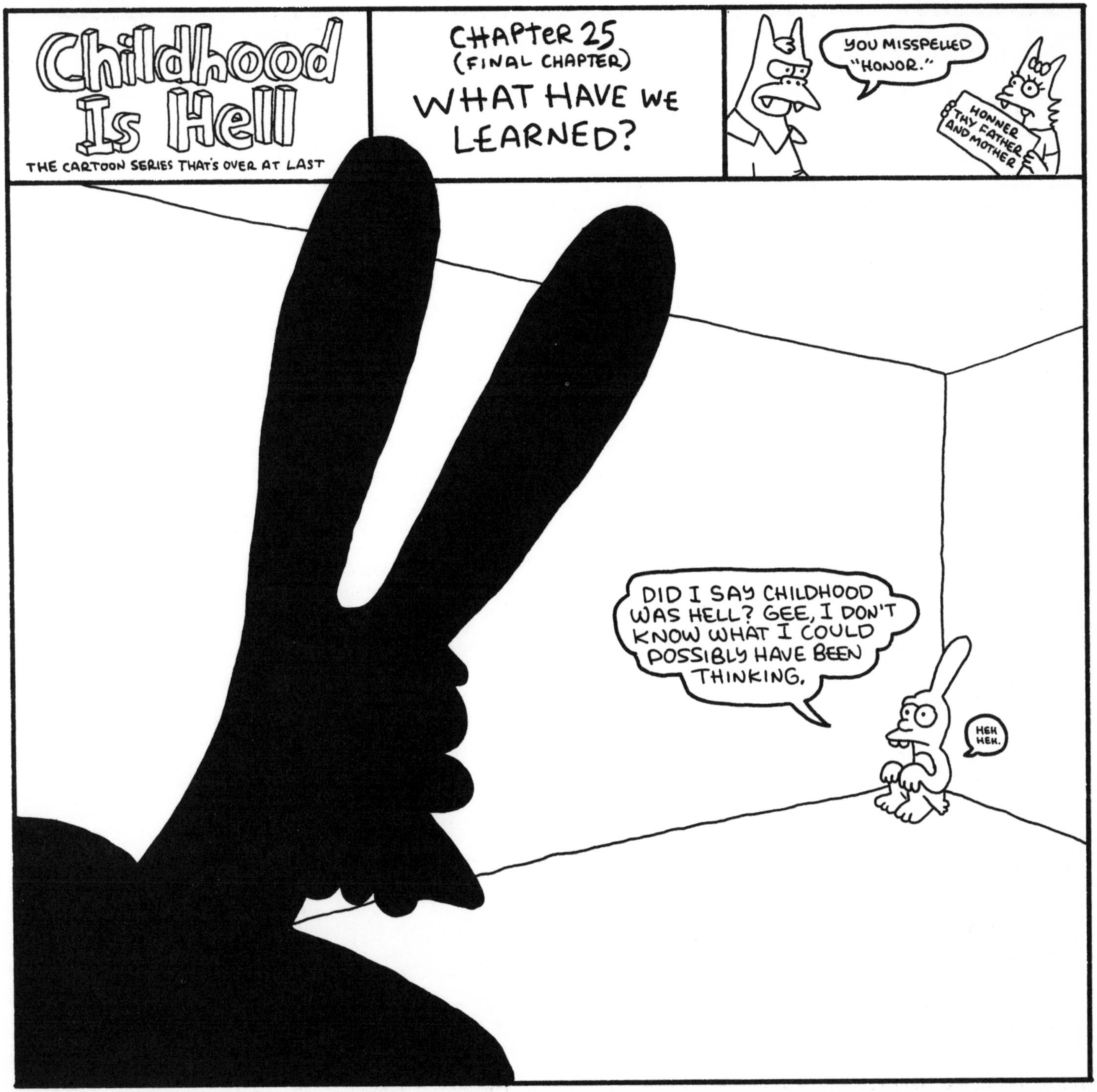
Childhood Is Hell
THE CARTOON SERIES THAT'S OVER AT LAST
CHAPTER 25
(FINAL CHAPTER)
WHAT HAVE WE LEARNED?
YOU MISSPELLED "HONOR."
HONNER THY FATHER AND MOTHER
DID I SAY CHILDHOOD WAS HELL? GEE, I DON'T KNOW WHAT I COULD POSSIBLY HAVE BEEN THINKING.
HEH HEH.

LIFE IN HELL

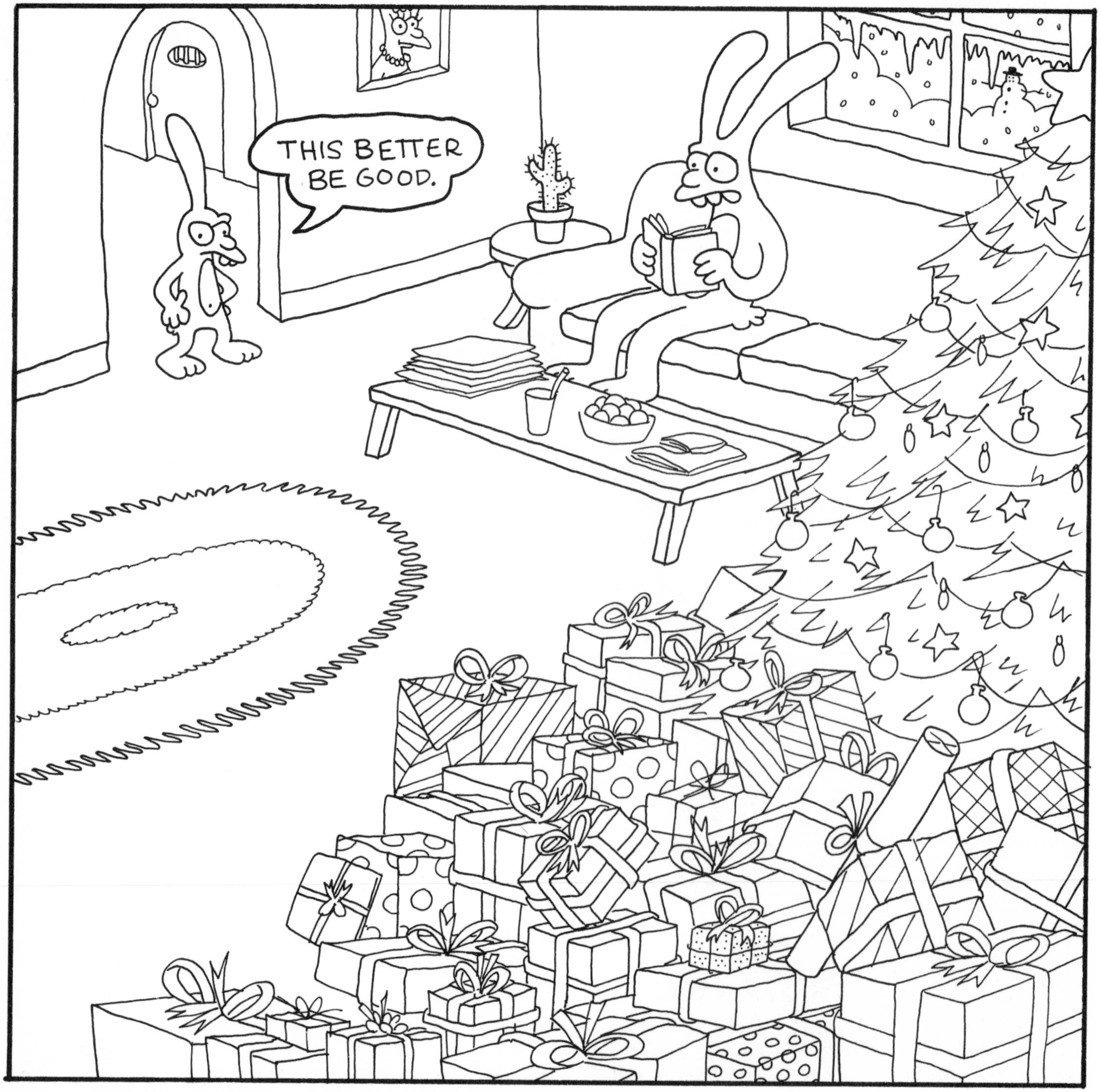
THIS BETTER BE GOOD.

XMAS IS HELL

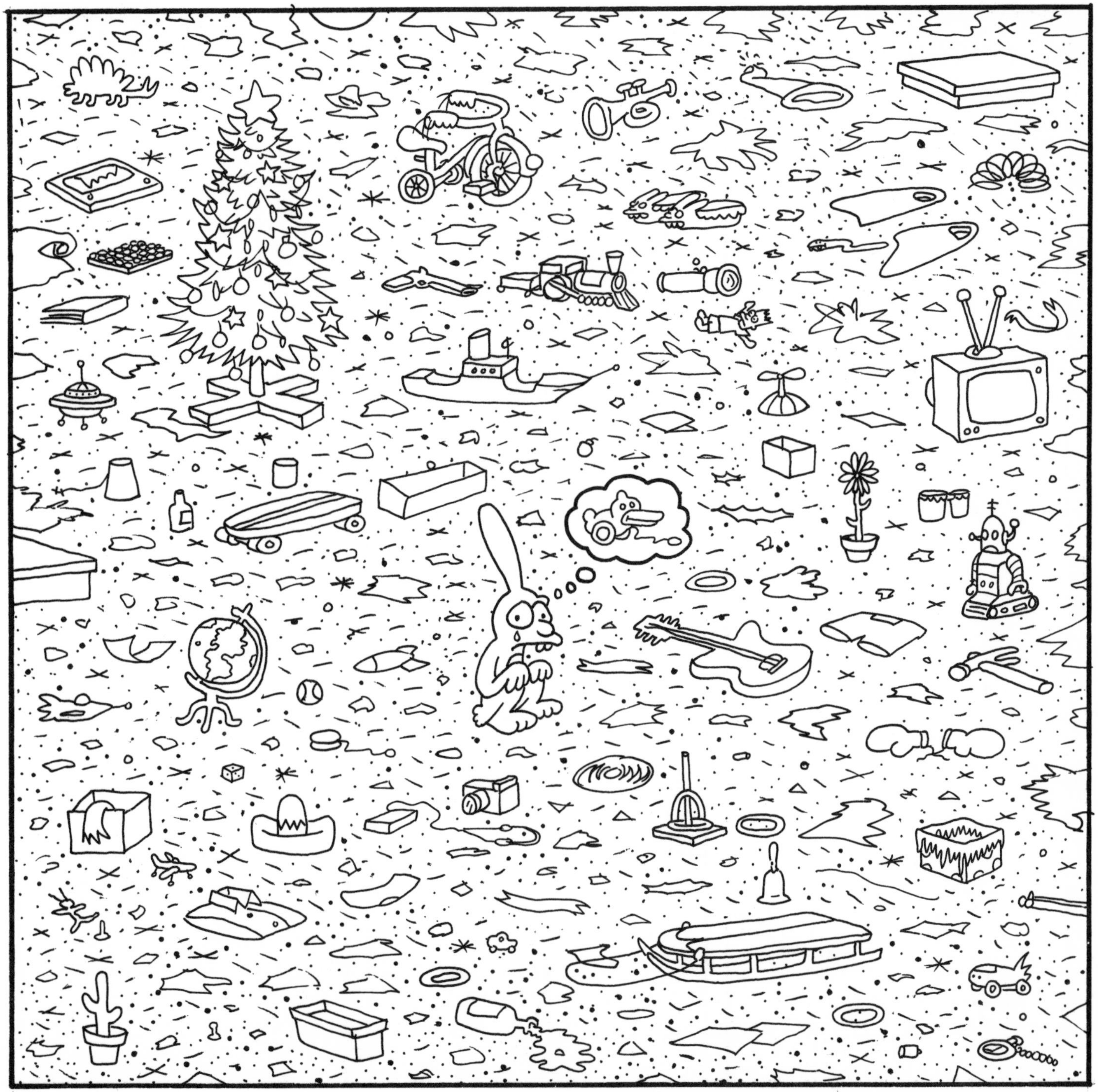

LIFE IN Hell

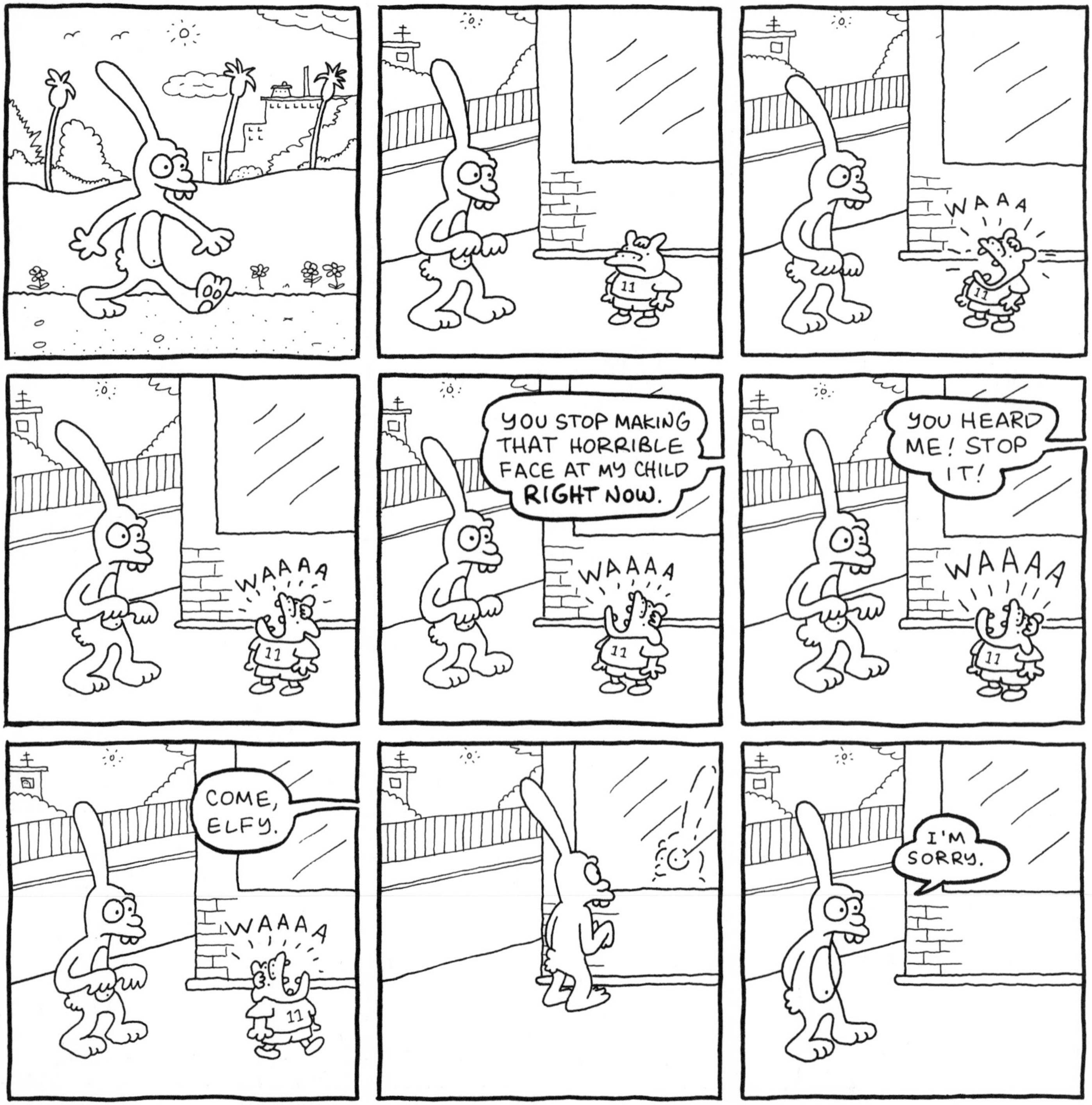

WAAA
WAAAA
YOU STOP MAKING THAT HORRIBLE FACE AT MY CHILD **RIGHT** NOW.
WAAAA
YOU HEARD ME! STOP IT!
WAAAA
COME, ELFY.
WAAAA
I'M SORRY.

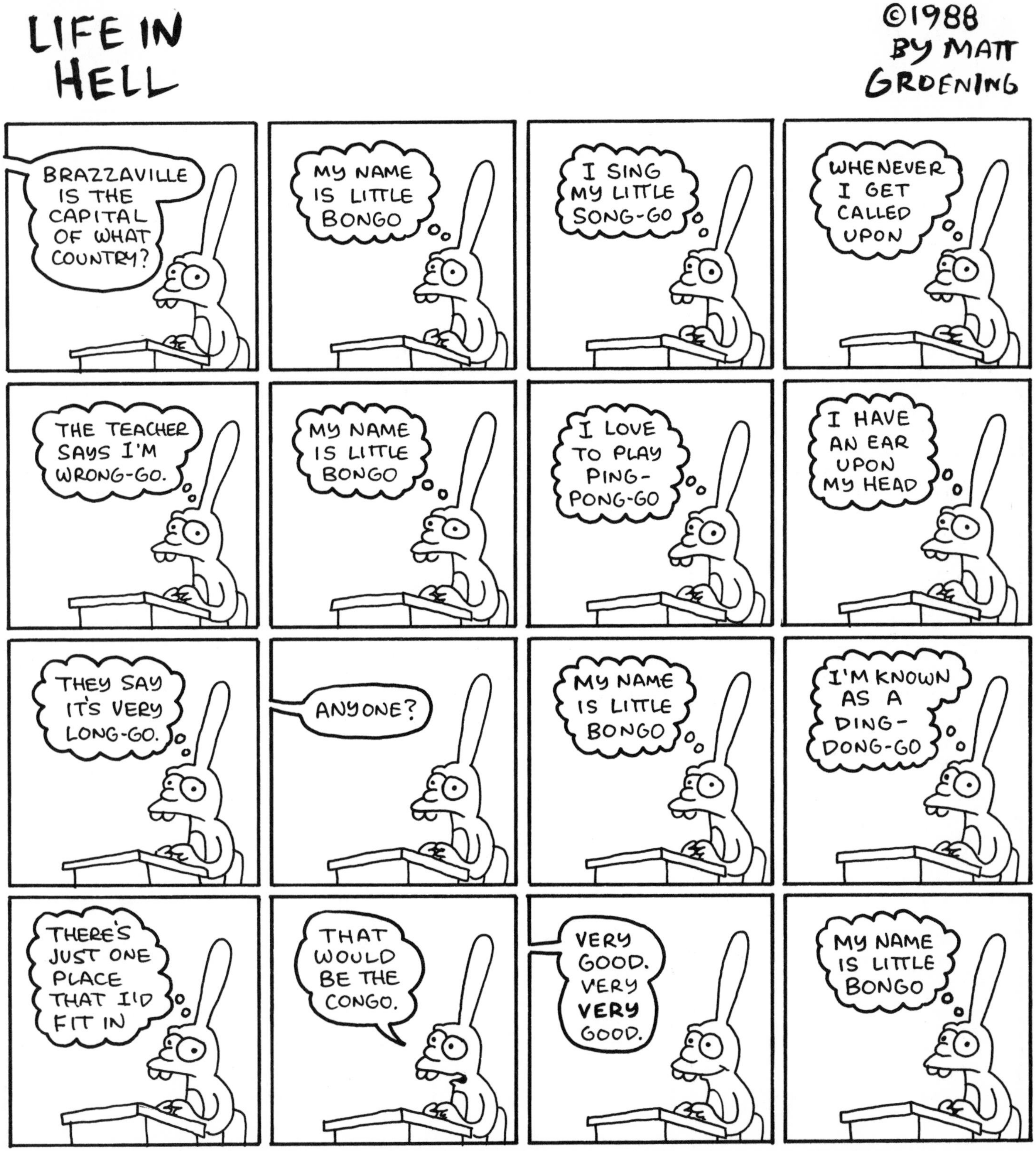
LIFE IN HELL
©1988 BY MATT GROENING
BRAZZAVILLE IS THE CAPITAL OF WHAT COUNTRY?
MY NAME IS LITTLE BONGO
I SING MY LITTLE SONG-GO
WHENEVER I GET CALLED UPON
THE TEACHER SAYS I'M WRONG-GO.
MY NAME IS LITTLE BONGO
I LOVE TO PLAY PING-PONG-GO
I HAVE AN EAR UPON MY HEAD
THEY SAY IT'S VERY LONG-GO.
ANYONE?
MY NAME IS LITTLE BONGO
I'M KNOWN AS A DING-DONG-GO
THERE'S JUST ONE PLACE THAT I'D FIT IN
THAT WOULD BE THE CONGO.
VERY GOOD. VERY VERY GOOD.
MY NAME IS LITTLE BONGO

LIFE IN HELL

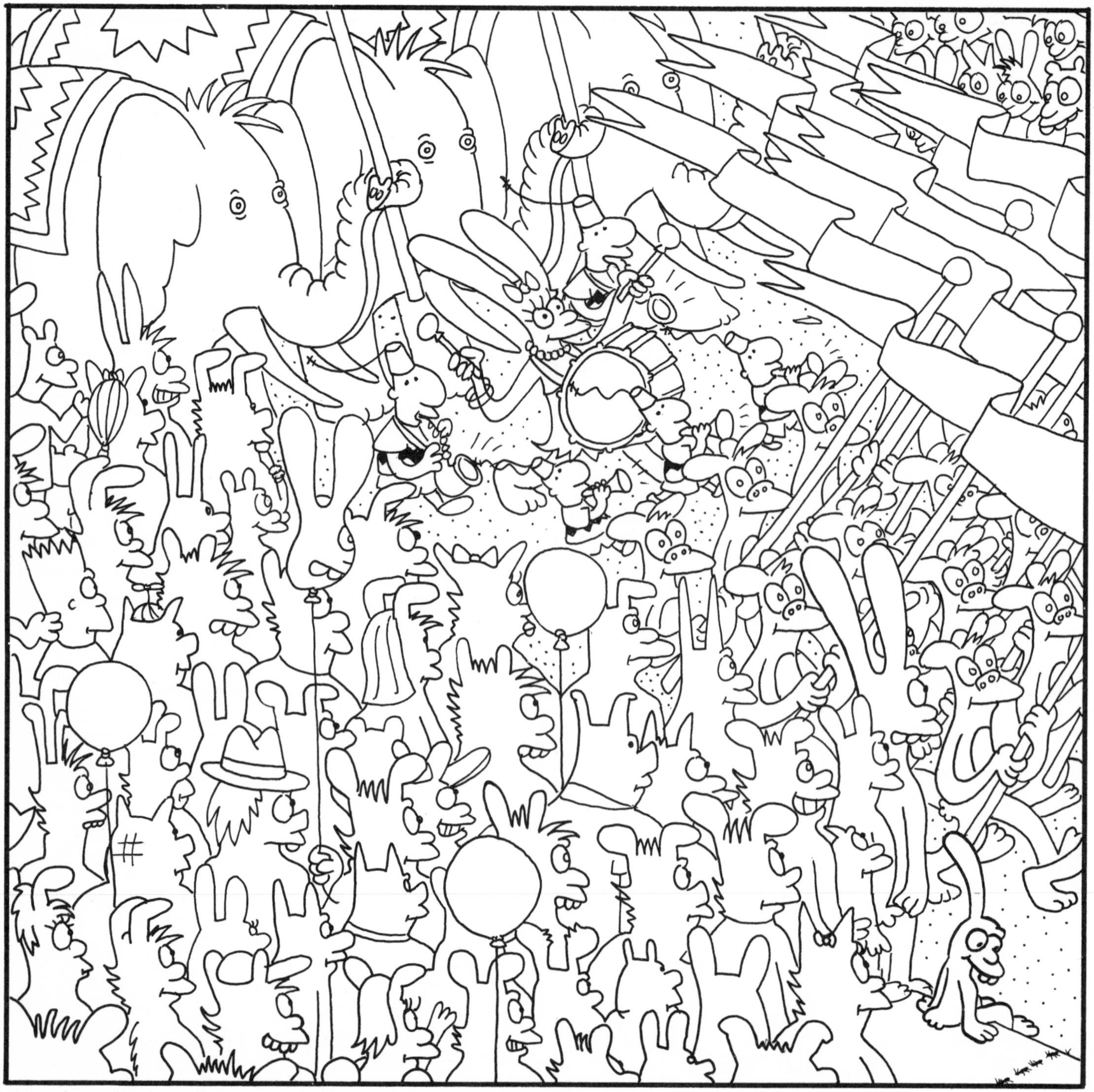

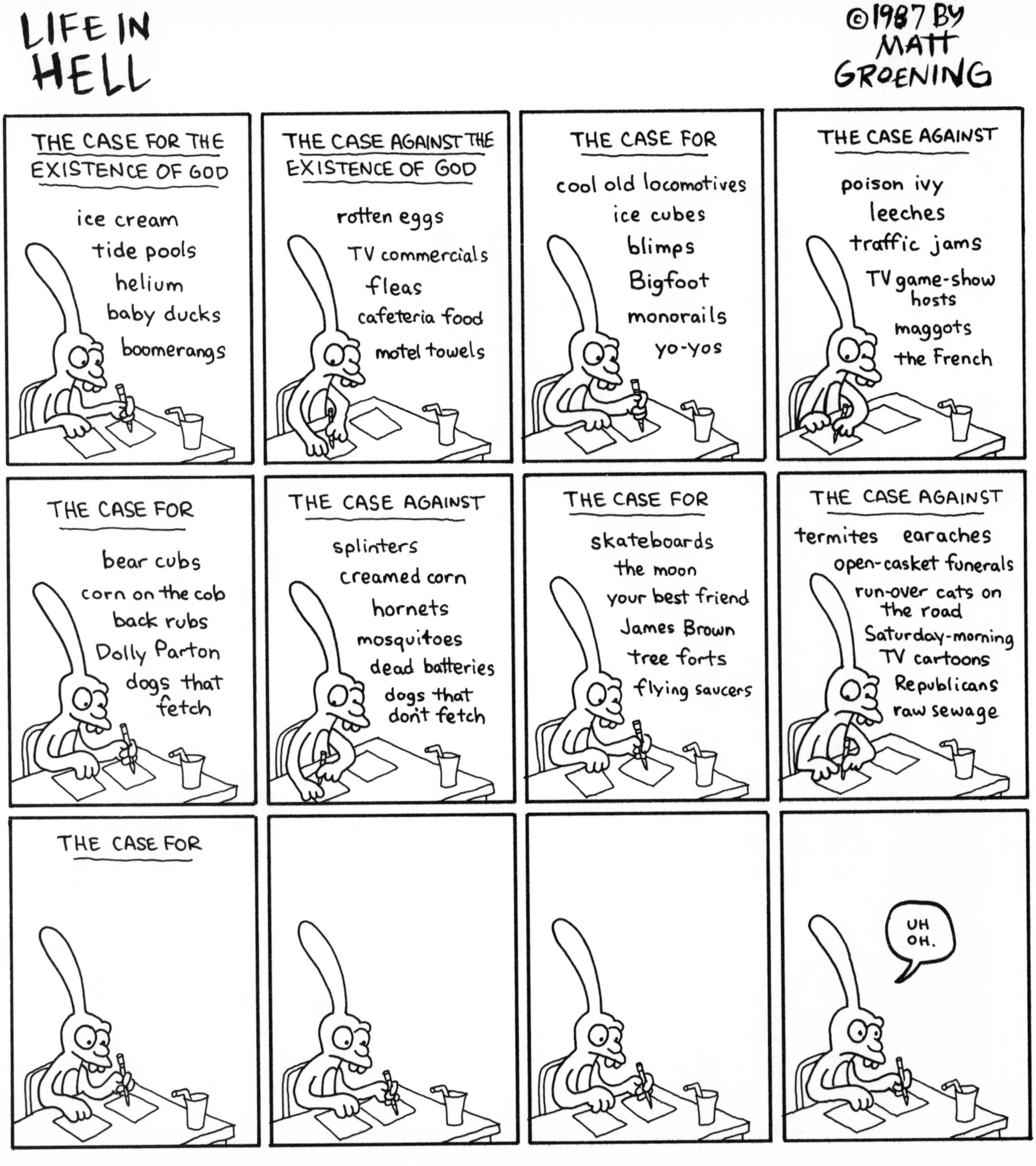
LIFE IN HELL
©1987 BY MATT GROENING
THE CASE FOR THE EXISTENCE OF GOD
ice cream
tide pools
helium
baby ducks
boomerangs
THE CASE AGAINST THE EXISTENCE OF GOD
rotten eggs
TV commercials
fleas
cafeteria food
motel towels
THE CASE FOR
cool old locomotives
ice cubes
blimps
Bigfoot
monorails
yo-yos
THE CASE AGAINST
poison ivy
leeches
traffic jams
TV game-show hosts
maggots
the French
THE CASE FOR
bear cubs
corn on the cob
back rubs
Dolly Parton
dogs that fetch
THE CASE AGAINST
splinters
creamed corn
hornets
mosquitoes
dead batteries
dogs that don't fetch
THE CASE FOR
skateboards
the moon
your best friend
James Brown
tree forts
flying saucers
THE CASE AGAINST
termites
earaches
open-casket funerals
run-over cats on the road
Saturday-morning TV cartoons
Republicans
raw sewage
THE CASE FOR
UH OH.

LIFE IN HELL

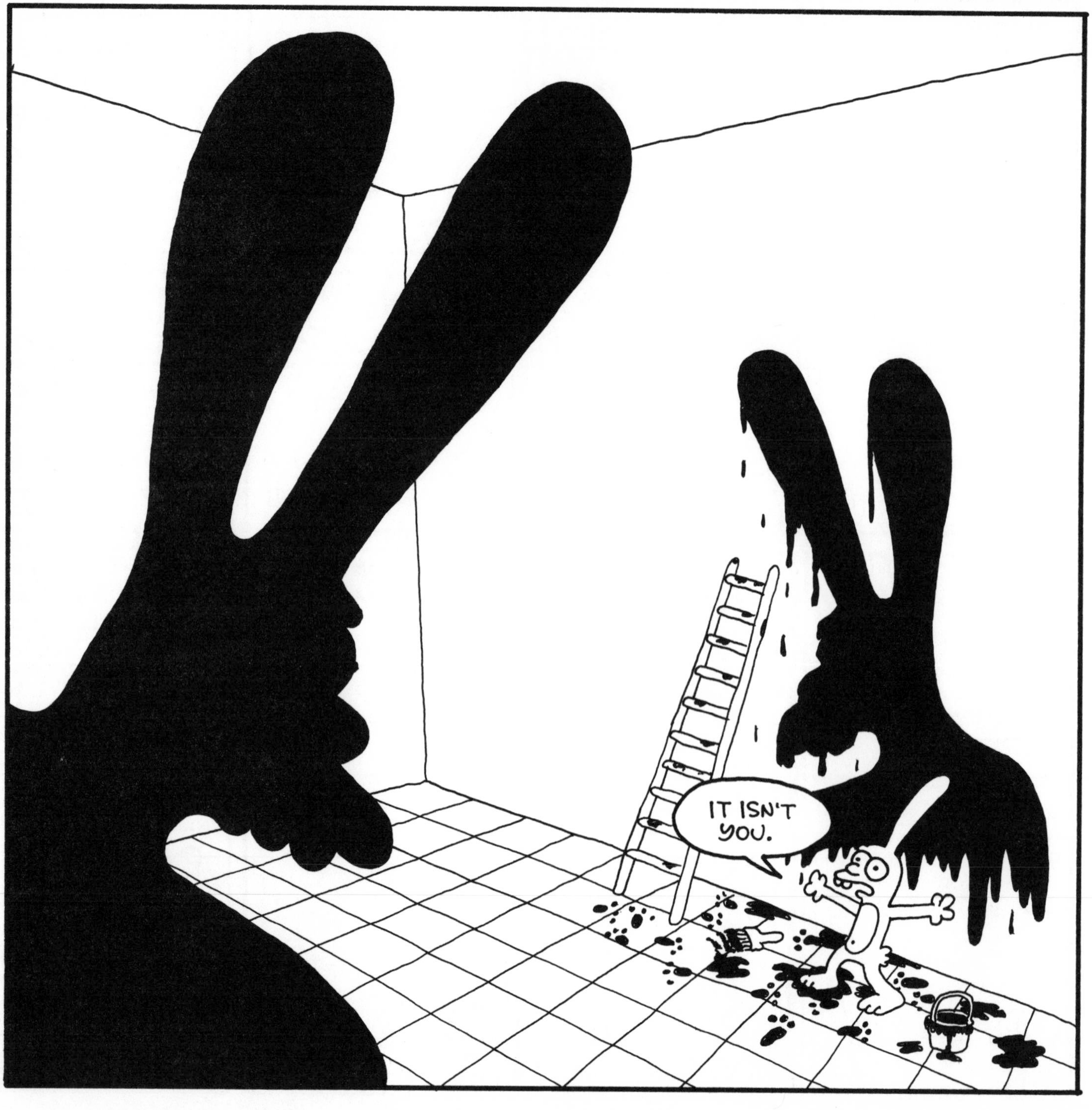
IT ISN'T YOU.

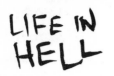

LIFE IN HELL

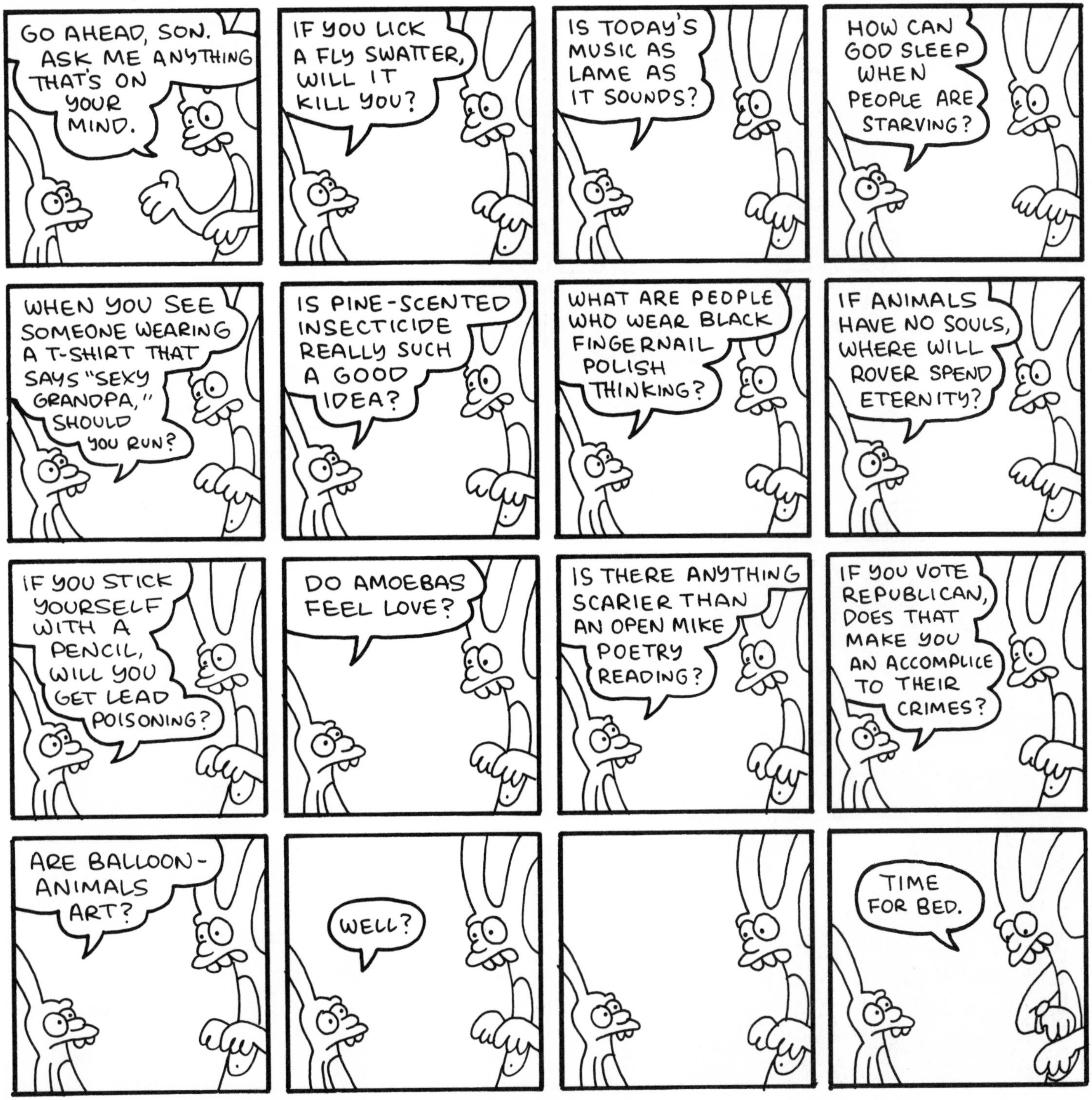
GO AHEAD, SON. ASK ME ANYTHING THAT'S ON YOUR MIND.
IF YOU LICK A FLY SWATTER, WILL IT KILL YOU?
IS TODAY'S MUSIC AS LAME AS IT SOUNDS?
HOW CAN GOD SLEEP WHEN PEOPLE ARE STARVING?
WHEN YOU SEE SOMEONE WEARING A T-SHIRT THAT SAYS "SEXY GRANDPA," SHOULD YOU RUN?
IS PINE-SCENTED INSECTICIDE REALLY SUCH A GOOD IDEA?
WHAT ARE PEOPLE WHO WEAR BLACK FINGERNAIL POLISH THINKING?
IF ANIMALS HAVE NO SOULS, WHERE WILL ROVER SPEND ETERNITY?
IF YOU STICK YOURSELF WITH A PENCIL, WILL YOU GET LEAD POISONING?
DO AMOEBAS FEEL LOVE?
IS THERE ANYTHING SCARIER THAN AN OPEN MIKE POETRY READING?
IF YOU VOTE REPUBLICAN, DOES THAT MAKE YOU AN ACCOMPLICE TO THEIR CRIMES?
ARE BALLOON-ANIMALS ART?
WELL?
TIME FOR BED.

LIFE IN HELL

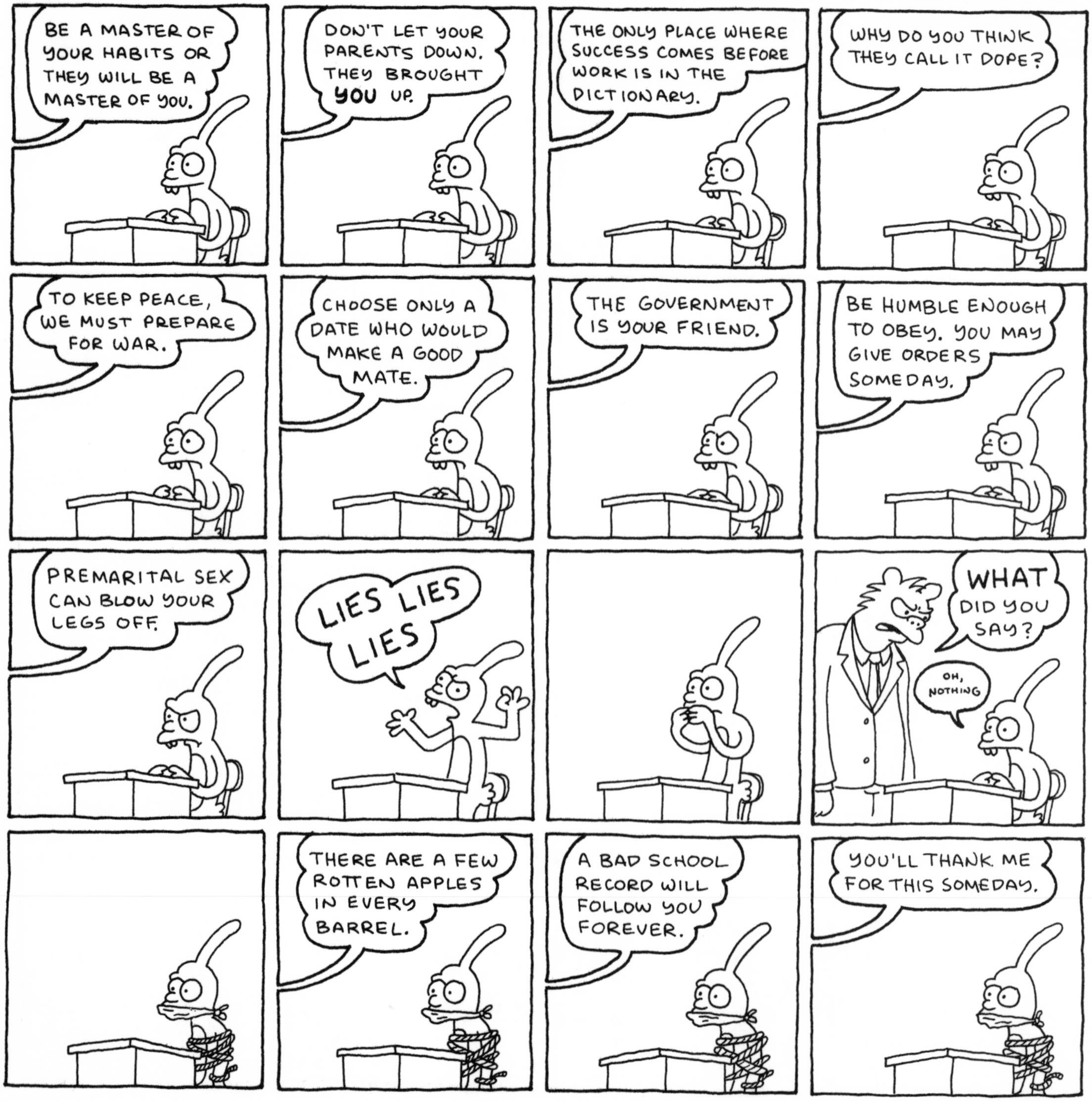
BE A MASTER OF YOUR HABITS OR THEY WILL BE A MASTER OF YOU.
DON'T LET YOUR PARENTS DOWN. THEY BROUGHT **YOU** UP.
THE ONLY PLACE WHERE SUCCESS COMES BEFORE WORK IS IN THE DICTIONARY.
WHY DO YOU THINK THEY CALL IT DOPE?
TO KEEP PEACE, WE MUST PREPARE FOR WAR.
CHOOSE ONLY A DATE WHO WOULD MAKE A GOOD MATE.
THE GOVERNMENT IS YOUR FRIEND.
BE HUMBLE ENOUGH TO OBEY. YOU MAY GIVE ORDERS SOMEDAY.
PREMARITAL SEX CAN BLOW YOUR LEGS OFF.
LIES LIES LIES LIES
WHAT DID YOU SAY?
OH, NOTHING
THERE ARE A FEW ROTTEN APPLES IN EVERY BARREL.
A BAD SCHOOL RECORD WILL FOLLOW YOU FOREVER.
YOU'LL THANK ME FOR THIS SOMEDAY.

LIFE IN HELL

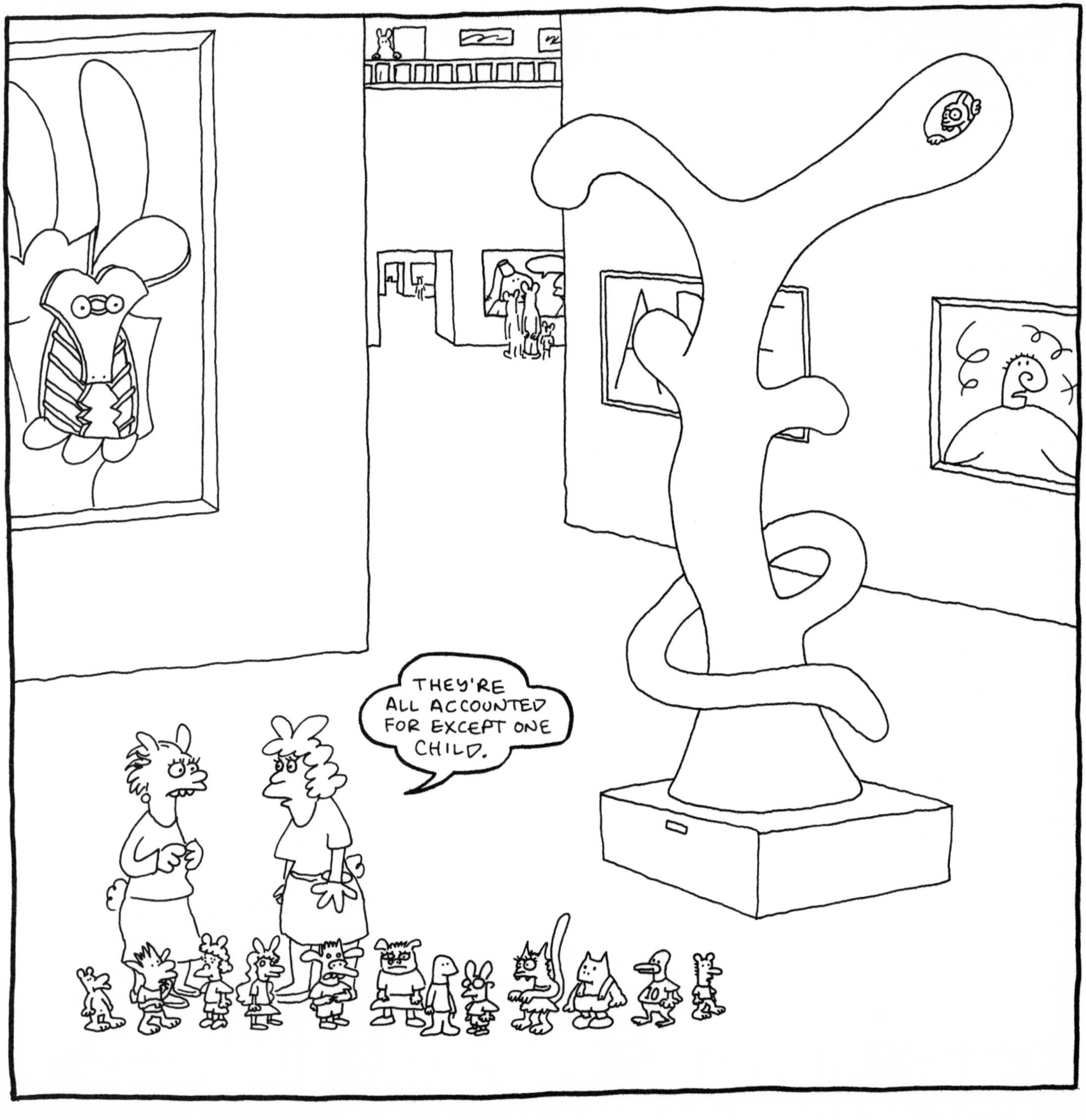
THEY'RE ALL ACCOUNTED FOR EXCEPT ONE CHILD.

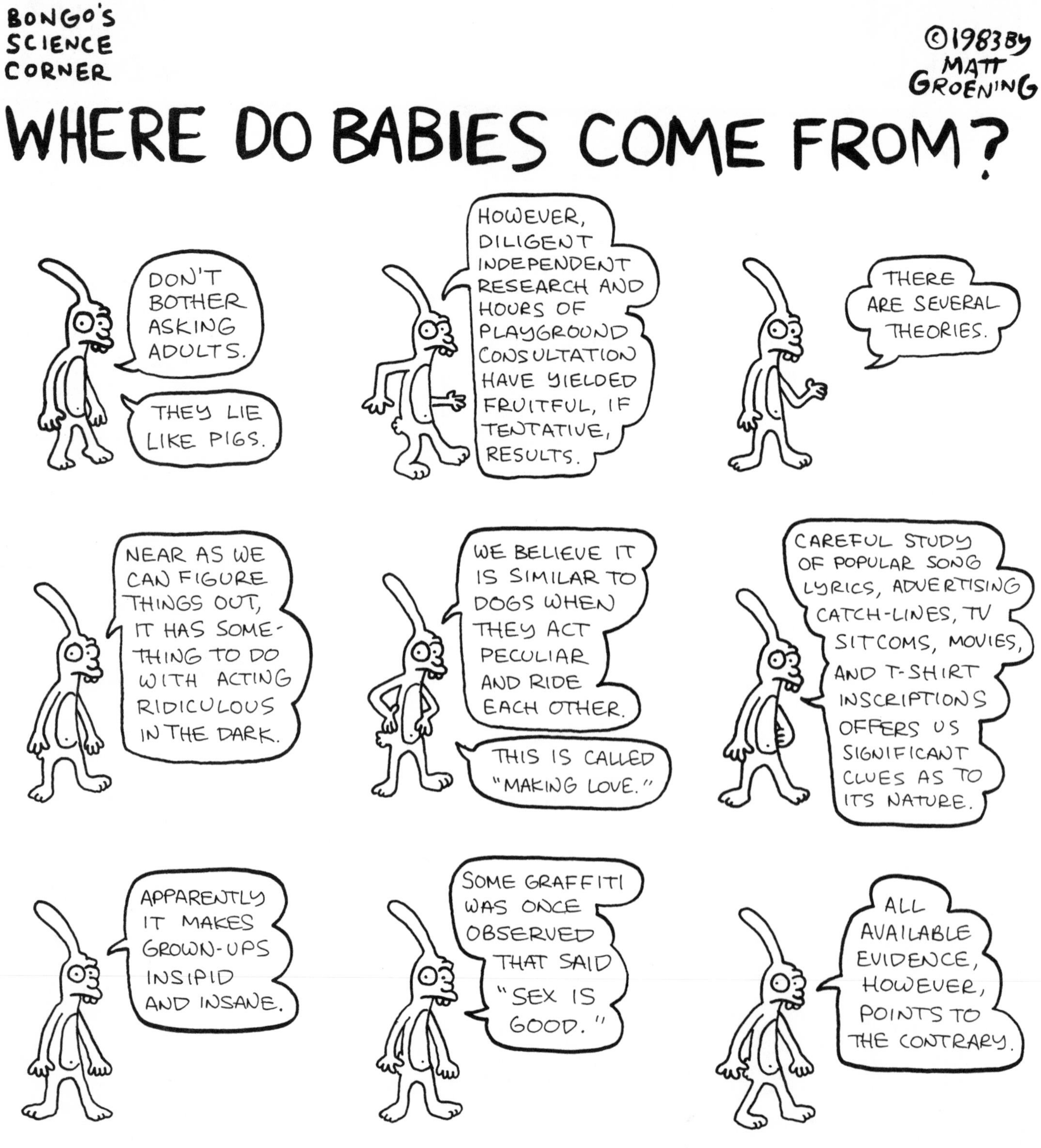

BONGO'S SCIENCE CORNER
©1983 BY MATT GROENING
WHERE DO BABIES COME FROM?
DON'T BOTHER ASKING ADULTS.
THEY LIE LIKE PIGS.
HOWEVER, DILIGENT INDEPENDENT RESEARCH AND HOURS OF PLAYGROUND CONSULTATION HAVE YIELDED FRUITFUL, IF TENTATIVE, RESULTS.
THERE ARE SEVERAL THEORIES.
NEAR AS WE CAN FIGURE THINGS OUT, IT HAS SOMETHING TO DO WITH ACTING RIDICULOUS IN THE DARK.
WE BELIEVE IT IS SIMILAR TO DOGS WHEN THEY ACT PECULIAR AND RIDE EACH OTHER.
THIS IS CALLED "MAKING LOVE."
CAREFUL STUDY OF POPULAR SONG LYRICS, ADVERTISING CATCH-LINES, TV SITCOMS, MOVIES, AND T-SHIRT INSCRIPTIONS OFFERS US SIGNIFICANT CLUES AS TO ITS NATURE.
APPARENTLY IT MAKES GROWN-UPS INSIPID AND INSANE.
SOME GRAFFITI WAS ONCE OBSERVED THAT SAID "SEX IS GOOD."
ALL AVAILABLE EVIDENCE, HOWEVER, POINTS TO THE CONTRARY.

LIFE IN HELL

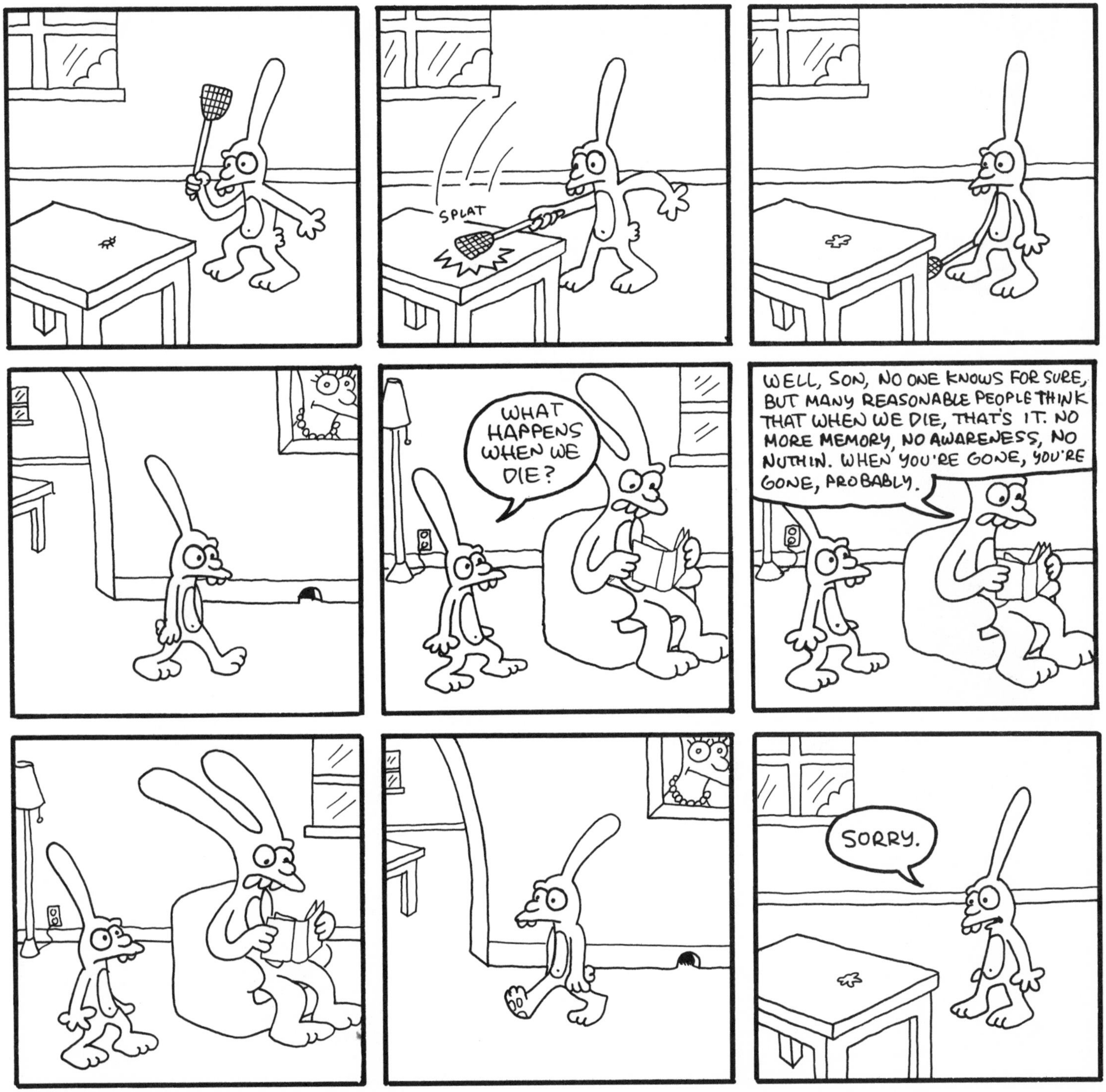
SPLAT
WHAT HAPPENS WHEN WE DIE?
WELL, SON, NO ONE KNOWS FOR SURE, BUT MANY REASONABLE PEOPLE THINK THAT WHEN WE DIE, THAT'S IT. NO MORE MEMORY, NO AWARENESS, NO NUTHIN. WHEN YOU'RE GONE, YOU'RE GONE, PROBABLY.
SORRY.

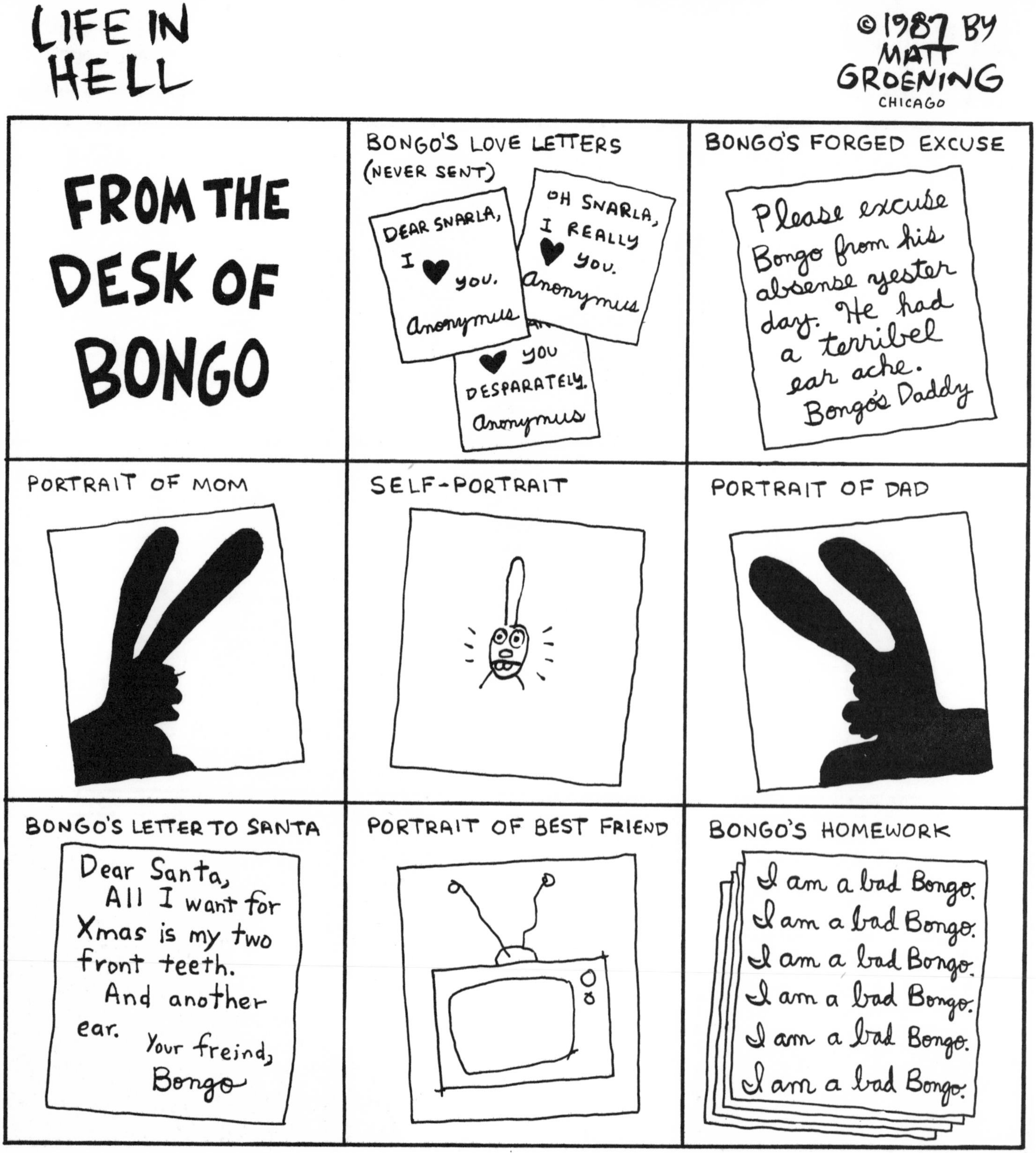

LIFE IN HELL
©1987 BY MATT GROENING CHICAGO
FROM THE DESK OF BONGO
BONGO'S LOVE LETTERS (NEVER SENT)
DEAR SNARLA, I ♥ YOU. Anonymus
OH SNARLA, I REALLY ♥ YOU. Anonymus
♥ YOU DESPARATELY. Anonymus
BONGO'S FORGED EXCUSE
Please excuse Bongo from his absense yester day. He had a terribel ear ache. Bongo's Daddy
PORTRAIT OF MOM
SELF-PORTRAIT
PORTRAIT OF DAD
BONGO'S LETTER TO SANTA
Dear Santa, All I want for Xmas is my two front teeth. And another ear. Your freind, Bongo
PORTRAIT OF BEST FRIEND
BONGO'S HOMEWORK
I am a bad Bongo.
I am a bad Bongo.
I am a bad Bongo.
I am a bad Bongo.
I am a bad Bongo.
I am a bad Bongo.

LIFE IN HELL

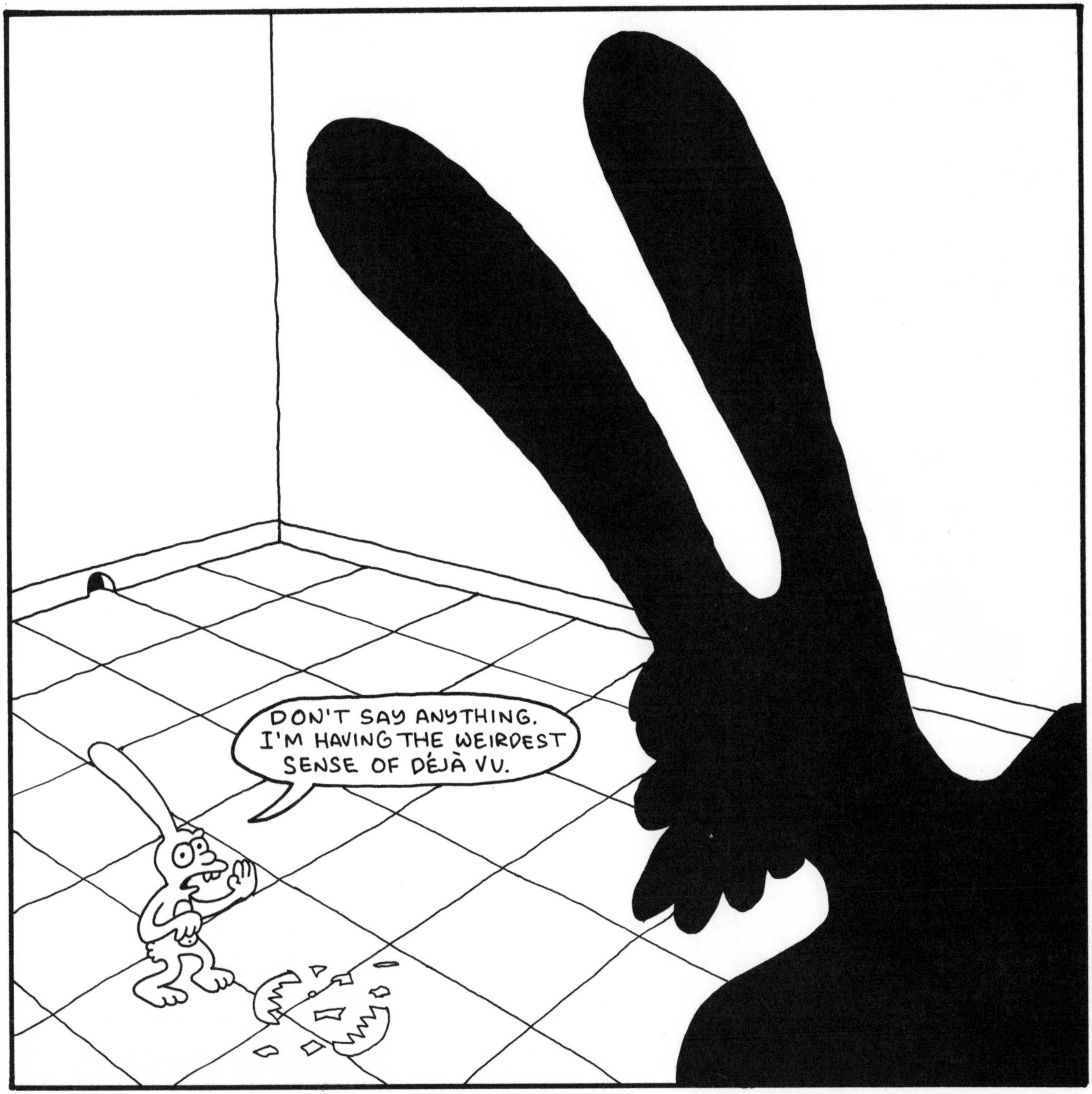
DON'T SAY ANYTHING. I'M HAVING THE WEIRDEST SENSE OF DÉJÀ VU.

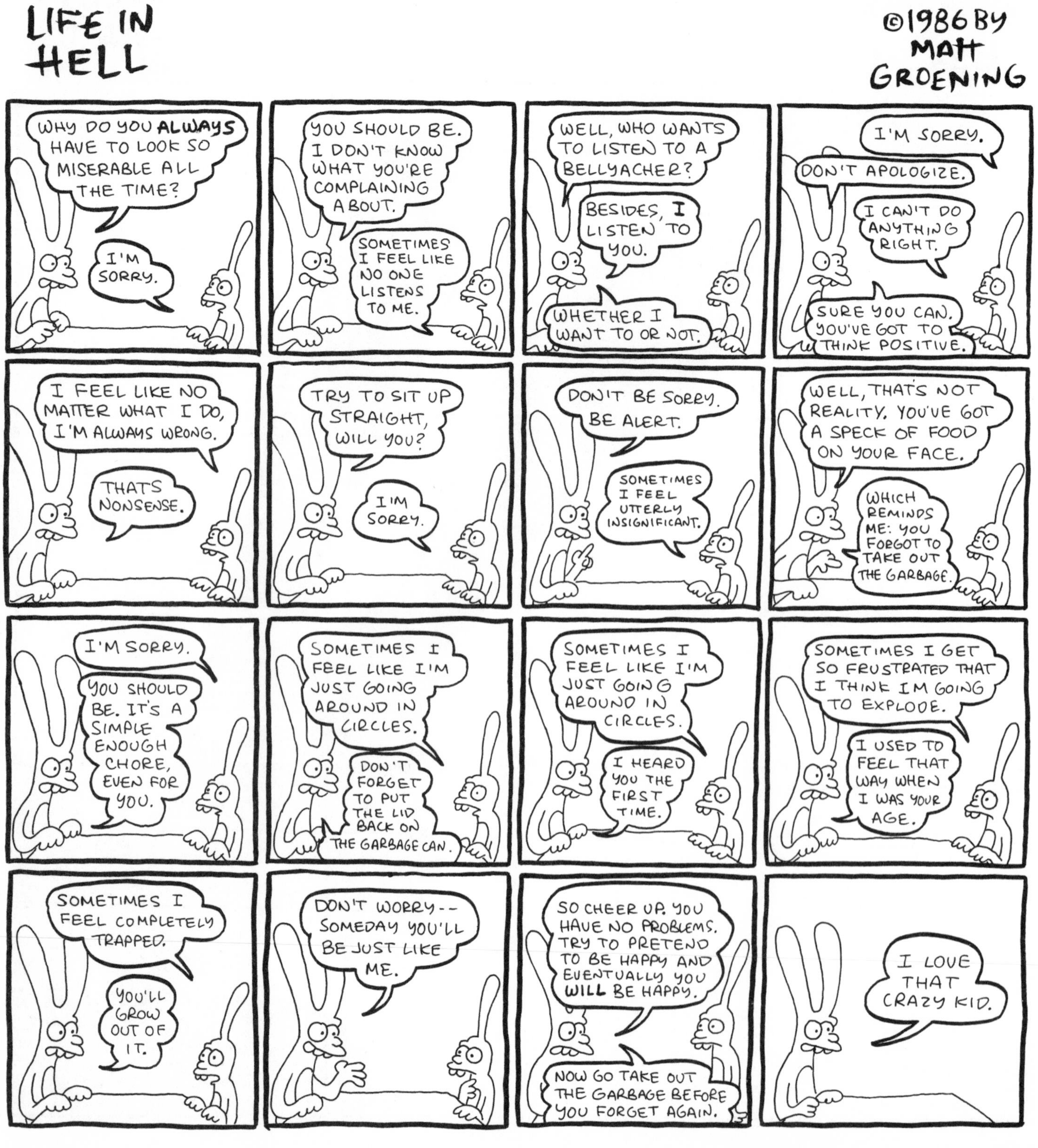

LIFE IN HELL
©1986 BY MATT GROENING
WHY DO YOU ALWAYS HAVE TO LOOK SO MISERABLE ALL THE TIME?
I'M SORRY.
YOU SHOULD BE. I DON'T KNOW WHAT YOU'RE COMPLAINING ABOUT.
SOMETIMES I FEEL LIKE NO ONE LISTENS TO ME.
WELL, WHO WANTS TO LISTEN TO A BELLYACHER?
BESIDES, I LISTEN TO YOU.
WHETHER I WANT TO OR NOT.
I'M SORRY.
DON'T APOLOGIZE.
I CAN'T DO ANYTHING RIGHT.
SURE YOU CAN. YOU'VE GOT TO THINK POSITIVE.
I FEEL LIKE NO MATTER WHAT I DO, I'M ALWAYS WRONG.
THAT'S NONSENSE.
TRY TO SIT UP STRAIGHT, WILL YOU?
I'M SORRY.
DON'T BE SORRY. BE ALERT.
SOMETIMES I FEEL UTTERLY INSIGNIFICANT.
WELL, THAT'S NOT REALITY. YOU'VE GOT A SPECK OF FOOD ON YOUR FACE.
WHICH REMINDS ME: YOU FORGOT TO TAKE OUT THE GARBAGE.
I'M SORRY.
YOU SHOULD BE. IT'S A SIMPLE ENOUGH CHORE, EVEN FOR YOU.
SOMETIMES I FEEL LIKE I'M JUST GOING AROUND IN CIRCLES.
DON'T FORGET TO PUT THE LID BACK ON THE GARBAGE CAN.
SOMETIMES I FEEL LIKE I'M JUST GOING AROUND IN CIRCLES.
I HEARD YOU THE FIRST TIME.
SOMETIMES I GET SO FRUSTRATED THAT I THINK I'M GOING TO EXPLODE.
I USED TO FEEL THAT WAY WHEN I WAS YOUR AGE.
SOMETIMES I FEEL COMPLETELY TRAPPED.
YOU'LL GROW OUT OF IT.
DON'T WORRY-- SOMEDAY YOU'LL BE JUST LIKE ME.
SO CHEER UP. YOU HAVE NO PROBLEMS. TRY TO PRETEND TO BE HAPPY AND EVENTUALLY YOU WILL BE HAPPY.
NOW GO TAKE OUT THE GARBAGE BEFORE YOU FORGET AGAIN.
I LOVE THAT CRAZY KID.

LIFE IN HELL

©1988 BY MATT GROENING

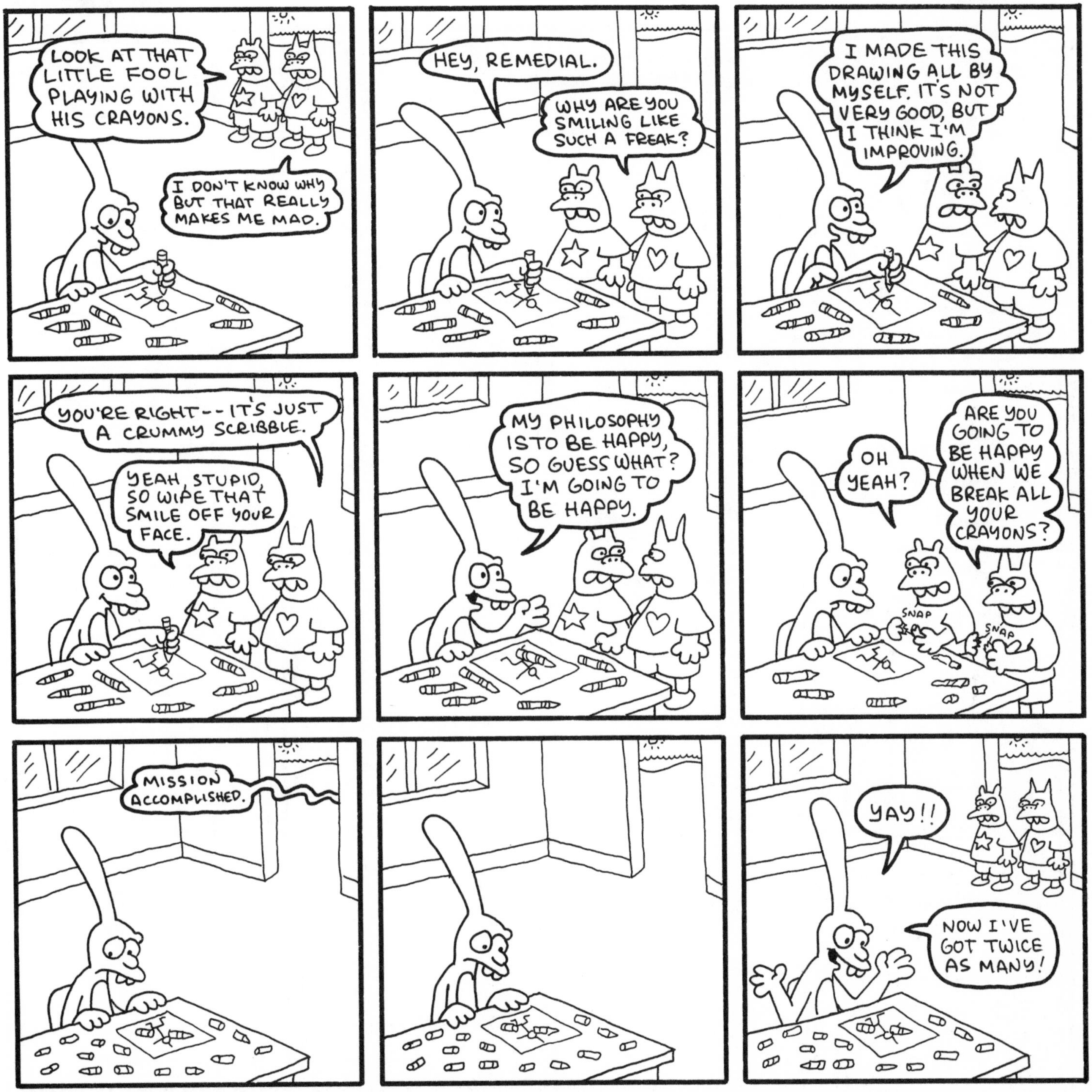
LOOK AT THAT LITTLE FOOL PLAYING WITH HIS CRAYONS.
I DON'T KNOW WHY BUT THAT REALLY MAKES ME MAD.
HEY, REMEDIAL.
WHY ARE YOU SMILING LIKE SUCH A FREAK?
I MADE THIS DRAWING ALL BY MYSELF. IT'S NOT VERY GOOD, BUT I THINK I'M IMPROVING.
YOU'RE RIGHT--IT'S JUST A CRUMMY SCRIBBLE.
YEAH, STUPID, SO WIPE THAT SMILE OFF YOUR FACE.
MY PHILOSOPHY IS TO BE HAPPY, SO GUESS WHAT? I'M GOING TO BE HAPPY.
OH YEAH?
ARE YOU GOING TO BE HAPPY WHEN WE BREAK ALL YOUR CRAYONS?
SNAP
SNAP
MISSION ACCOMPLISHED.
YAY!!
NOW I'VE GOT TWICE AS MANY!

LIFE IN HELL

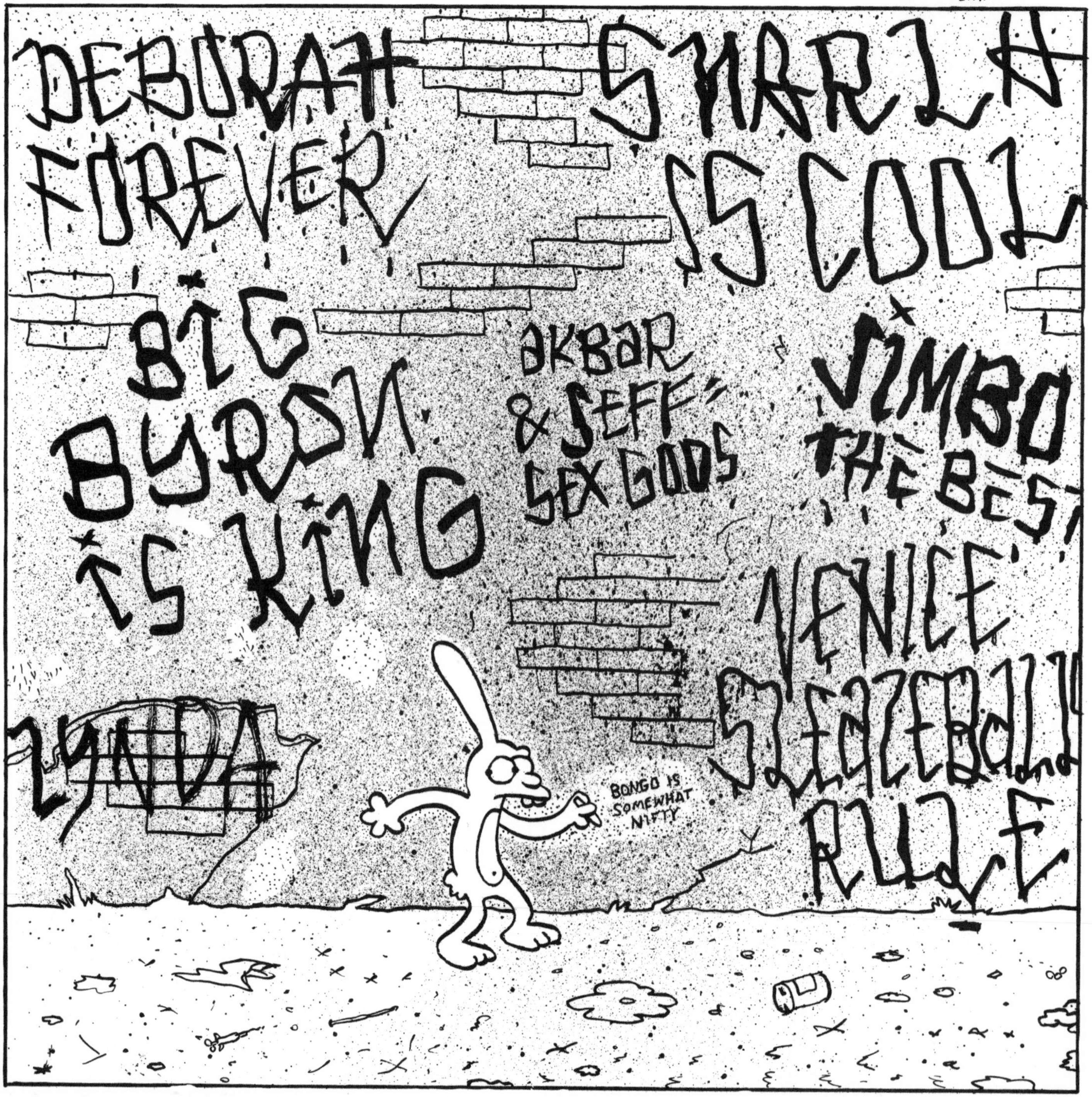
DEBORAH FOREVER
BIG BYRON IS KING
akbar & JEFF SEX GODS
JIMBO THE BEST
LYNDA
VENICE SLEAZEBALLS RULE
BONGO IS SOMEWHAT NIFTY

LIFE IN HELL

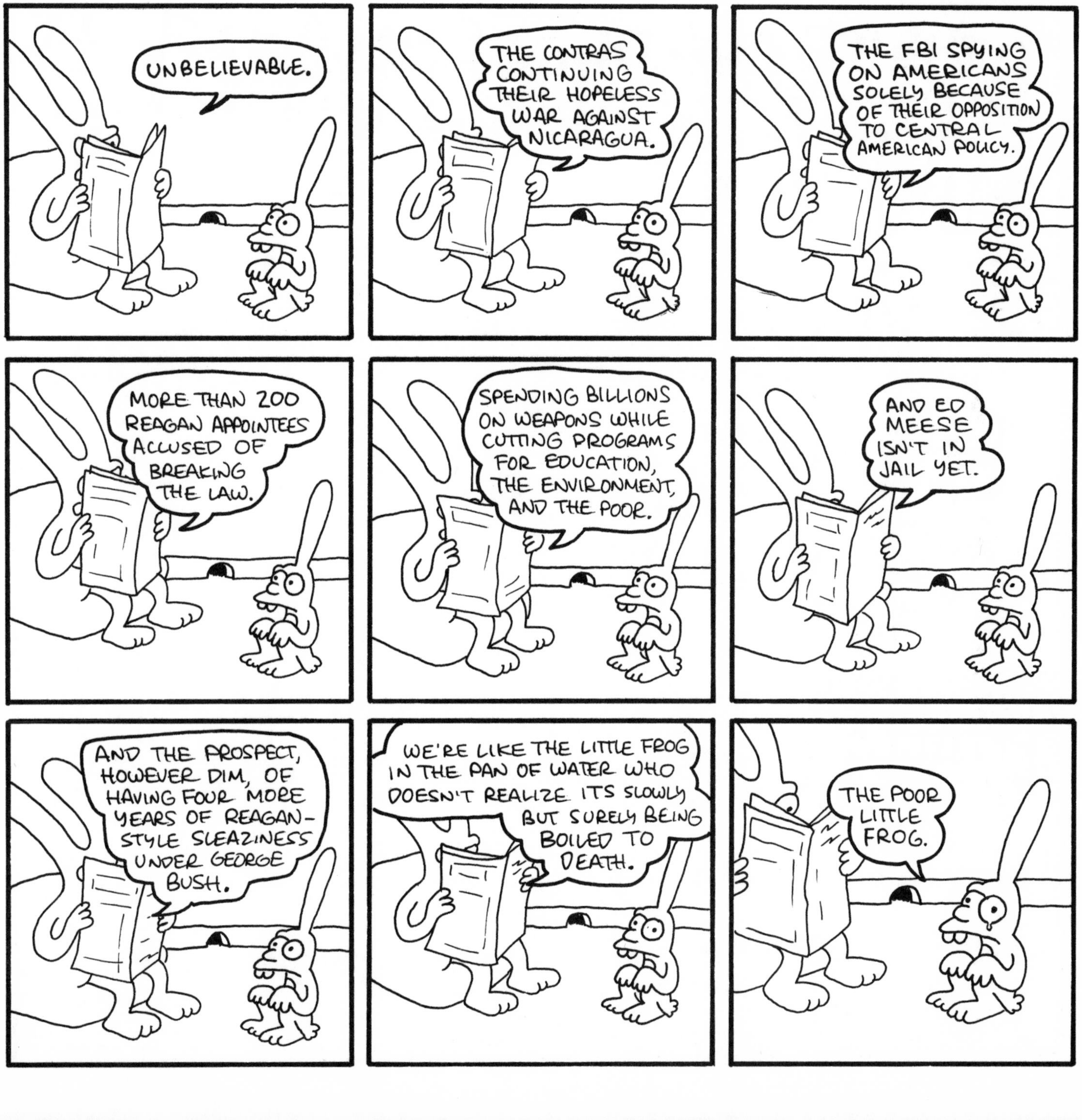
UNBELIEVABLE.
THE CONTRAS CONTINUING THEIR HOPELESS WAR AGAINST NICARAGUA.
THE FBI SPYING ON AMERICANS SOLELY BECAUSE OF THEIR OPPOSITION TO CENTRAL AMERICAN POLICY.
MORE THAN 200 REAGAN APPOINTEES ACCUSED OF BREAKING THE LAW.
SPENDING BILLIONS ON WEAPONS WHILE CUTTING PROGRAMS FOR EDUCATION, THE ENVIRONMENT, AND THE POOR.
AND ED MEESE ISN'T IN JAIL YET.
AND THE PROSPECT, HOWEVER DIM, OF HAVING FOUR MORE YEARS OF REAGAN-STYLE SLEAZINESS UNDER GEORGE BUSH.
WE'RE LIKE THE LITTLE FROG IN THE PAN OF WATER WHO DOESN'T REALIZE ITS SLOWLY BUT SURELY BEING BOILED TO DEATH.
THE POOR LITTLE FROG.

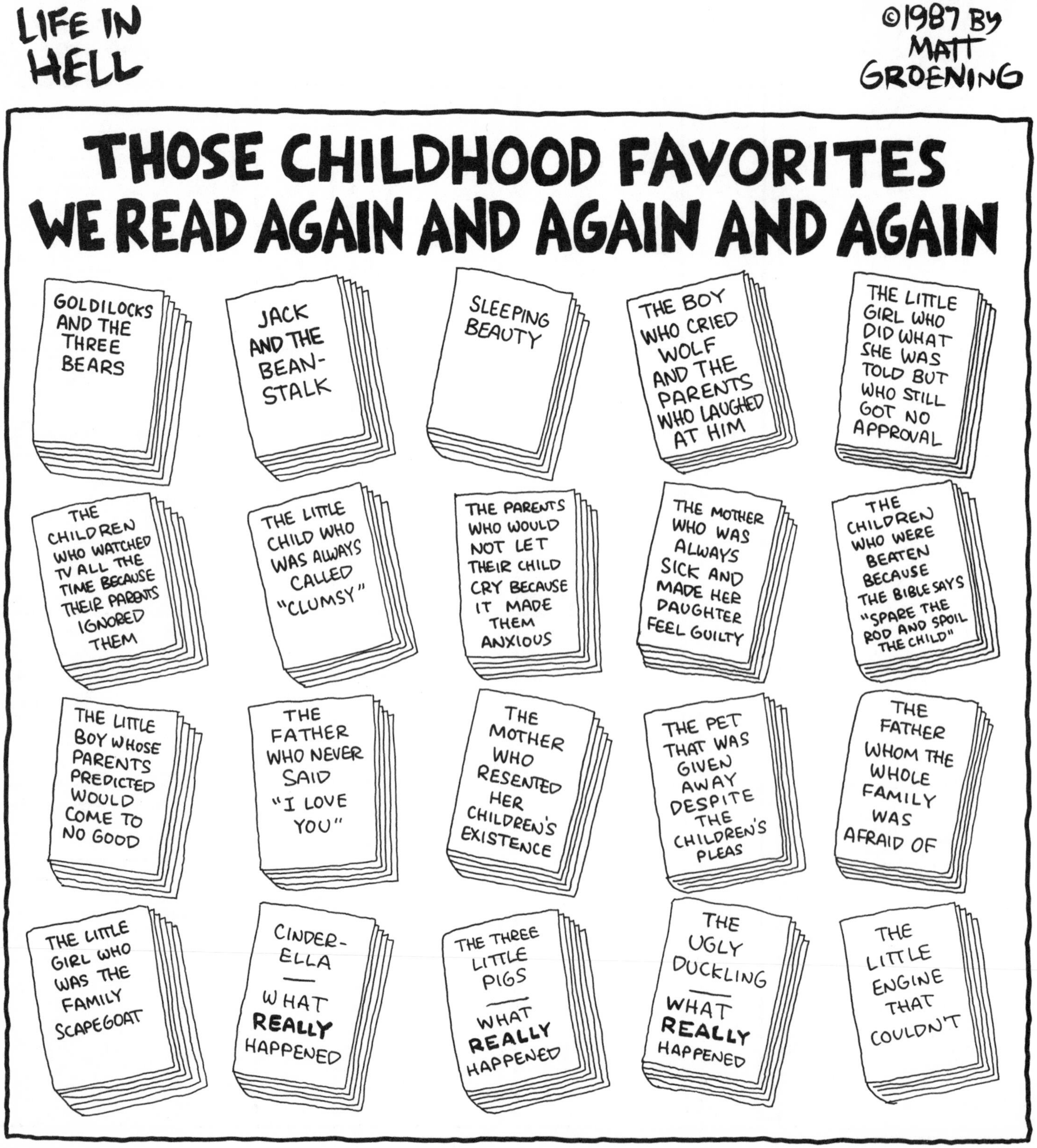
LIFE IN HELL
©1987 BY MATT GROENING
THOSE CHILDHOOD FAVORITES WE READ AGAIN AND AGAIN AND AGAIN
GOLDILOCKS AND THE THREE BEARS
JACK AND THE BEAN-STALK
SLEEPING BEAUTY
THE BOY WHO CRIED WOLF AND THE PARENTS WHO LAUGHED AT HIM
THE LITTLE GIRL WHO DID WHAT SHE WAS TOLD BUT WHO STILL GOT NO APPROVAL
THE CHILDREN WHO WATCHED TV ALL THE TIME BECAUSE THEIR PARENTS IGNORED THEM
THE LITTLE CHILD WHO WAS ALWAYS CALLED "CLUMSY"
THE PARENTS WHO WOULD NOT LET THEIR CHILD CRY BECAUSE IT MADE THEM ANXIOUS
THE MOTHER WHO WAS ALWAYS SICK AND MADE HER DAUGHTER FEEL GUILTY
THE CHILDREN WHO WERE BEATEN BECAUSE THE BIBLE SAYS "SPARE THE ROD AND SPOIL THE CHILD"
THE LITTLE BOY WHOSE PARENTS PREDICTED WOULD COME TO NO GOOD
THE FATHER WHO NEVER SAID "I LOVE YOU"
THE MOTHER WHO RESENTED HER CHILDREN'S EXISTENCE
THE PET THAT WAS GIVEN AWAY DESPITE THE CHILDREN'S PLEAS
THE FATHER WHOM THE WHOLE FAMILY WAS AFRAID OF
THE LITTLE GIRL WHO WAS THE FAMILY SCAPEGOAT
CINDER-ELLA — WHAT REALLY HAPPENED
THE THREE LITTLE PIGS — WHAT REALLY HAPPENED
THE UGLY DUCKLING — WHAT REALLY HAPPENED
THE LITTLE ENGINE THAT COULDN'T

LIFE IN HELL

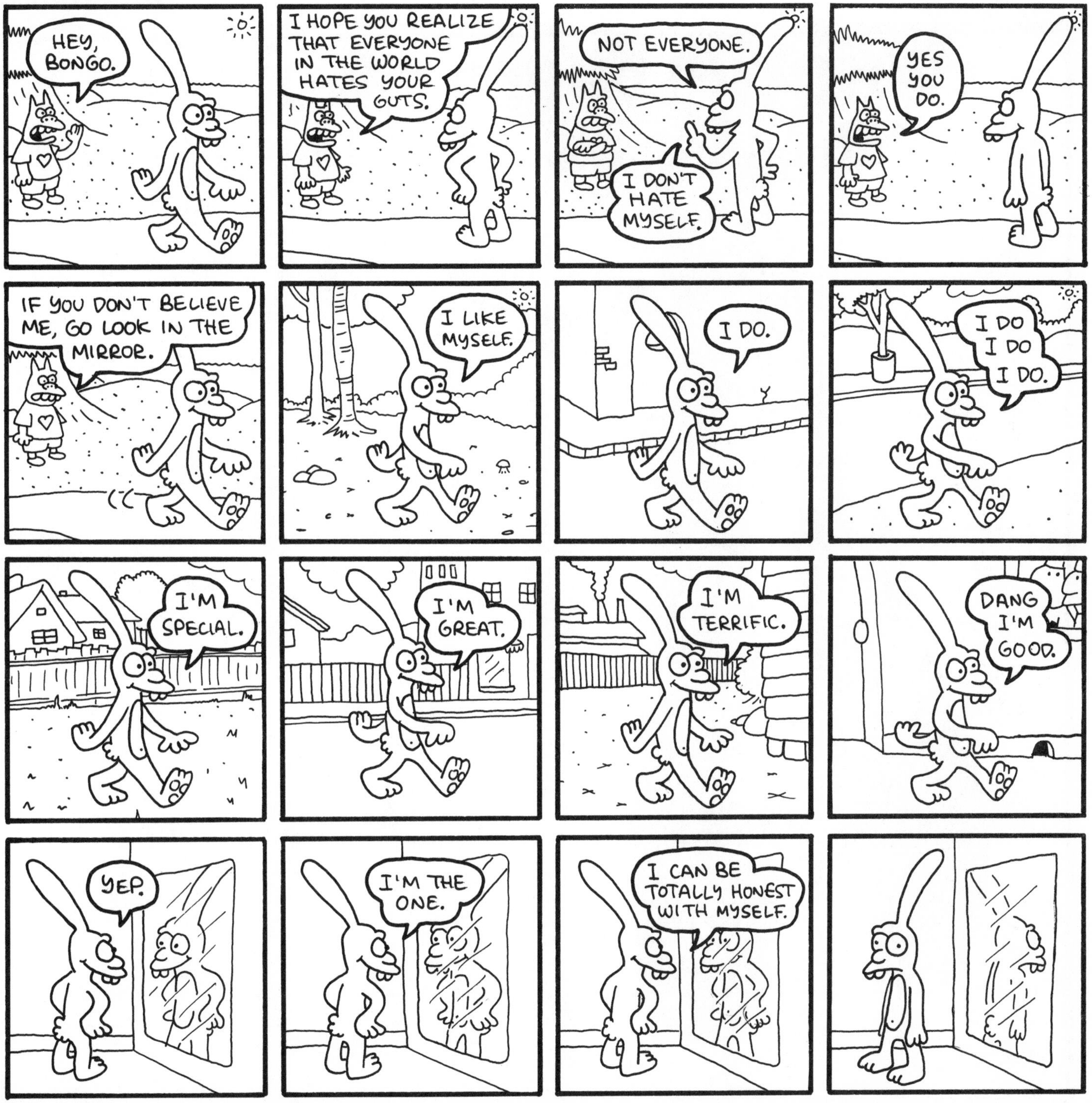

HEY, BONGO.
I HOPE YOU REALIZE THAT EVERYONE IN THE WORLD HATES YOUR GUTS.
NOT EVERYONE.
I DON'T HATE MYSELF.
YES YOU DO.
IF YOU DON'T BELIEVE ME, GO LOOK IN THE MIRROR.
I LIKE MYSELF.
I DO.
I DO I DO I DO.
I'M SPECIAL.
I'M GREAT.
I'M TERRIFIC.
DANG I'M GOOD.
YEP.
I'M THE ONE.
I CAN BE TOTALLY HONEST WITH MYSELF.

LIFE IN HELL

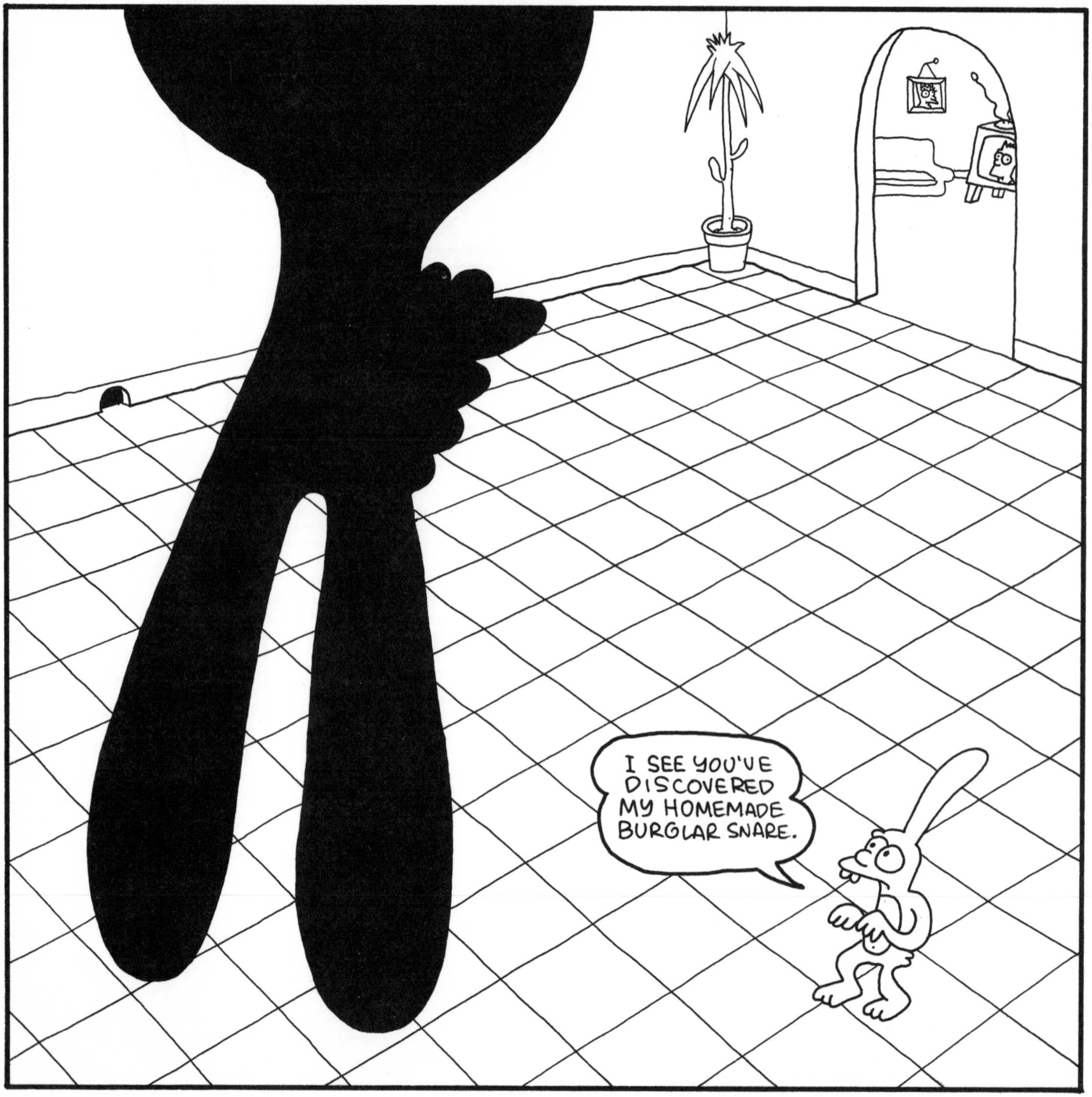
I SEE YOU'VE DISCOVERED MY HOMEMADE BURGLAR SNARE.